T0355429

Number Puzzles

Michellejoy Hughes

OXFORD
UNIVERSITY PRESS

UNIVERSITY PRESS

Great Clarendon Street, Oxford, OX2 6DP, United Kingdom

Oxford University Press is a department of the University of Oxford.
It furthers the University's objective of excellence in research, scholarship,
and education by publishing worldwide. Oxford is a registered trade mark
of Oxford University Press in the UK and in certain other countries

Text © Oxford University Press 2018

Author: Michellejoy Hughes

The moral rights of the author have been asserted

First published in 2019

British Library Cataloguing in Publication Data
Data available

978-0-19--276954-1

10 9 8 7 6 5

Paper used in the production of this book is a natural, recyclable product
made from wood grown in sustainable forests. The manufacturing process
conforms to the environmental regulations of the country of origin.

Printed in China

Acknowledgements

Cover illustrations by Holly Fulbrook
Page make-up and illustrations by James W. Hunter

Although we have made every effort to trace and contact all copyright
holders before publication this has not been possible in all cases. If notified,
the publisher will rectify any errors or omissions at the earliest opportunity.

Links to third party websites are provided by Oxford in good faith and for
information only. Oxford disclaims any responsibility for the materials
contained in any third party website referenced in this work.

The manufacturer's authorised representative in the EU for product
safety is Oxford University Press España S.A. of el Parque Empresarial
San Fernando de Henares, Avenida de Castilla, 2 – 28830 Madrid
(www.oup.es/en).

Hi Puzzle Fan,

Are you ready to test your brain power? Sharpen your pencil and let's kick-start your brain with these number puzzle challenges.

There are puzzles here for everyone so if you like…

- secret codes and sequences

- number puzzles and clever tricks

- mazes and meanderings

- triples, groups and pairs

…there will be lots of things here you will love.

Along the way you will meet some interesting characters, ponder over riddles and crack plenty of codes.

How to use this book

In this book there are three sections of puzzles –
warm-up, intermediate and tricky. They get more
challenging as you progress through the book.
Follow the simple introduction at the start of each
puzzle and use a pencil in case you need to rub
anything out. At the end of each section add up your
score to discover your puzzle power.

By the end of the book you will be an ace
codebreaker, a dab hand at mazes and a wizard
at number puzzles. That means increased number
power, too!

You can find the answers at the back of the book,
but don't look until you have completed the puzzles!
A notepad is included on some pages in case you
need space to help you work out the answer.

 We've put in some puzzle pointers to give
you a clue so look out for the jigsaw symbol.

So what are
you waiting for?
Let's get going on
some number puzzle
challenges...

Number facts

Here is a list of useful terms that can help you solve some of the puzzles.

Prime numbers

A prime number is a whole number that can only be divided by itself and 1. The number 1 is not a prime number. The number 2 is the only even prime number. Here are the first ten prime numbers: 2, 3, 5, 7, 11, 13, 17, 19, 23, 29.

Square numbers

A square number is a number multiplied by itself. A little '2' after the number shows it is squared:

$1^2 = 1 \times 1 = 1$ $\qquad$ $2^2 = 2 \times 2 = 4$

$3^2 = 3 \times 3 = 9$ $\qquad$ $4^2 = 4 \times 4 = 16$

$5^2 = 5 \times 5 = 25$ $\qquad$ $6^2 = 6 \times 6 = 36$

$7^2 = 7 \times 7 = 49$ $\qquad$ $8^2 = 8 \times 8 = 64$

$9^2 = 9 \times 9 = 81$ $\qquad$ $10^2 = 10 \times 10 = 100$

$11^2 = 11 \times 11 = 121$ $\qquad$ $12^2 = 12 \times 12 = 144$

$13^2 = 13 \times 13 = 169$ $\qquad$ $14^2 = 14 \times 14 = 196$

Cube numbers

A cube number is a number multiplied by itself and then multiplied by itself again. A little '3' after the number shows it is cubed:

$1^3 = 1 \times 1 \times 1 = 1$ $2^3 = 2 \times 2 \times 2 = 8$

$3^3 = 3 \times 3 \times 3 = 27$ $4^3 = 4 \times 4 \times 4 = 64$

$5^3 = 5 \times 5 \times 5 = 125$ $6^3 = 6 \times 6 \times 6 = 216$

$7^3 = 7 \times 7 \times 7 = 343$ $8^3 = 8 \times 8 \times 8 = 512$

$9^3 = 9 \times 9 \times 9 = 729$ $10^3 = 10 \times 10 \times 10 = 1000$

Triangular numbers

A triangular number is a number sequence from a pattern of dots that form a triangle. We can add another row of dots and count all the dots to find the next number in the sequence.

1

1

3

$1 + 2 = 3$

6

$1 + 2 + 3 = 6$

10

$1 + 2 + 3 + 4 = 10$

15

$1 + 2 + 3 + 4 + 5 = 15$

21

$1 + 2 + 3 + 4 + 5 + 6 = 21$

Fibonacci sequence

The Fibonacci sequence is 0, 1, 1, 2, 3, 5, 8, 13, 21, 34 ... To find the next number in the sequence, we add up the two numbers before it.

$0 + 1 = 1$ $1 + 1 = 2$ $1 + 2 = 3$ $2 + 3 = 5$

$3 + 5 = 8$ $5 + 8 = 13$ $8 + 13 = 21$

The first two numbers are 0 and 1. When we add these together, it makes a total of 1. So the next number in the sequence is also 1.

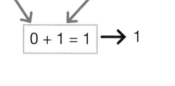

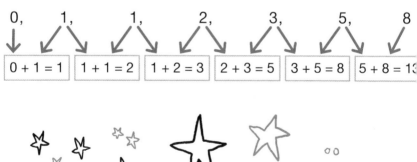

Warm-up puzzles

1 Sandcastles 1

In a number pyramid, the numbers on the lower levels determine the numbers above them. Follow the pattern to fill in the missing numbers on the sandcastles.

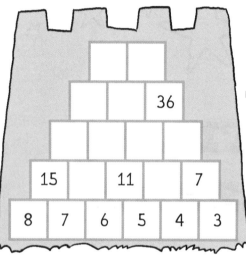

8 + 7 = 15

Puzzle Pointer

Add each number on the bottom line to the number next to it to work out the numbers on the line above.

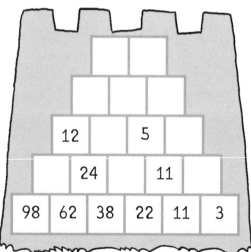

Puzzle Pointer

Find the difference between each number on the bottom line and the number next to it to work out the numbers on the line above.

Monster maths 1

Solve these monster maths problems. There are lines for you to write notes on.

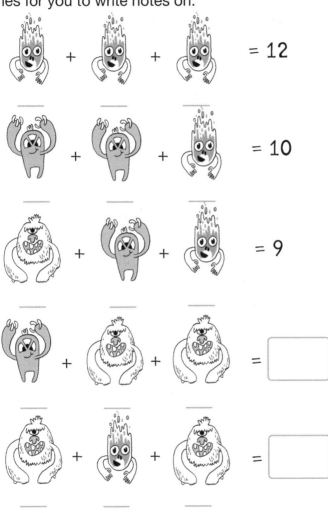

? Puzzle Pointer

Three monsters in the first row = 12 so what is the value of this type of monster? Take this number away from ten and divide by two to solve the next line down.

Puzzle Pointer

The **Number facts** on pages 5–8 will help you
with some of these sequences.

Complete the next two numbers in these sequences.
Then follow the instructions to find your key.

1.	5	10	15	20	25	☐	☐
2.	97	87	78	70	63	☐	☐
3.	120	105	90	75	60	☐	☐
4.	2	4	8	16	32	☐	☐
5.	144	121	100	81	64	☐	☐

6. Now add up your answers to make a
   three-digit number and write it here: ☐

7. Add up the three digits
   and write the number here: ☐

If the number is a prime number, circle Key A.
If it is not a prime number, circle Key B.

Key A   Key B

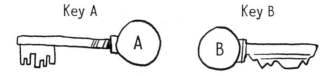

Warm-up

4 Zoo numbers

Add up the number of letters in each animal's name.
Count how many letters there are in each word,
then use the numbers to solve these animal maths
problems. The first one has been done for you.

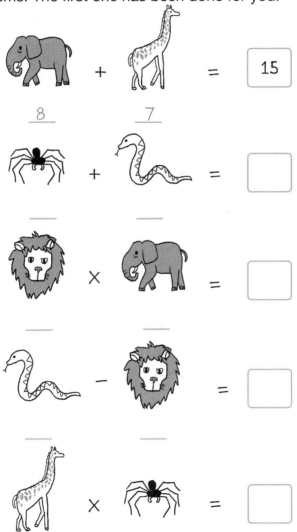

$$\text{elephant} + \text{giraffe} = \boxed{15}$$
$$8 \qquad\qquad 7$$

$$\text{spider} + \text{snake} = \boxed{}$$

$$\text{lion} \times \text{elephant} = \boxed{}$$

$$\text{snake} - \text{lion} = \boxed{}$$

$$\text{giraffe} \times \text{spider} = \boxed{}$$

Warm-up

Draw lines to connect shapes making sure the total number of sides of the two shapes adds up to 10.

- No line can touch another.

- You can only draw lines that are horizontal or vertical, not diagonal.

One has been done for you.

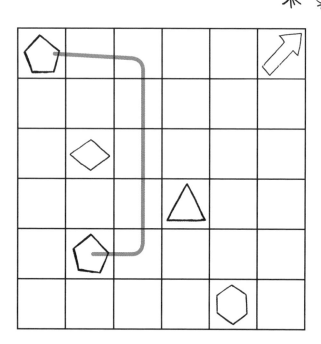

6 Secret codes

Use the code to work out the joke.

1	2	3	4	5	6	7	8	9
A	B	C	D	E	F	G	H	I

10	11	12	13	14	15	16	17	18
J	K	L	M	N	O	P	Q	R

19	20	21	22	23	24	25	26	27
S	T	U	V	W	X	T	Z	?

8 15 23   4 15 5 19   1

12 9 15 14   7 18 5 5 20

15 20 8 5 18   1 14 9 13 1 12 19 27

Pleased to eat you!

15

Warm-up

The fire fighters need to climb the ladders to reach the top of the house. Start at the bottom and complete the sums to climb up the ladders. Write the final number for each ladder in the top boxes.

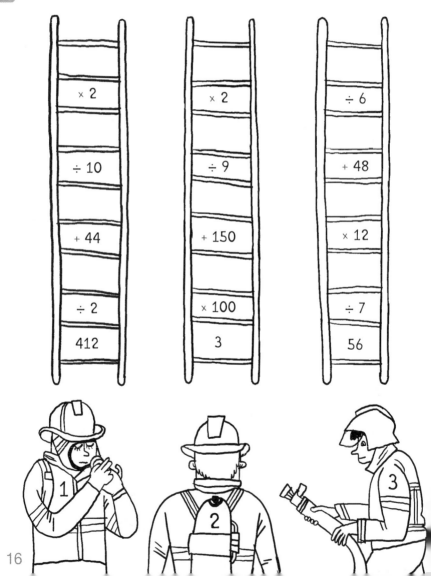

Ladder 1:
× 2
÷ 10
+ 44
÷ 2
412

Ladder 2:
× 2
÷ 9
+ 150
× 100
3

Ladder 3:
÷ 6
+ 48
× 12
÷ 7
56

These look like normal sentences but they are not!
Hidden between words or inside words are some
numbers. Draw a line under all the numbers you find.
The first one has been done for you.

1. Go outside i**f our** fire alarm rings.

2. I arrived too soon every morning.

3. We wound the thread on both reels.

4. I don't eat kulfi very often but I love
   the taste of it.

5. What is the weight of these parcels?

6. Check your answers even if you are sure.

Why not have a go
at making up your own
sentences with hidden
numbers in them?

9 Shade art 1

Shade in the following numbers. The remaining numbers will make a pattern.

- Shade in all numbers in the three times table.

- Shade in all the prime numbers.

- The **Number facts** on pages 5–8 will help you with prime numbers.

2	9	8	28	7	11
39	22	24	36	35	5
3	33	21	30	4	12
5	18	38	80	36	24
24	7	16	18	6	3
17	13	12	24	21	27
9	19	10	15	33	6

Now try this:

Ask your friend what the sum of the first five odd numbers is and say that you can add them up quicker than them. While they add up the numbers, all you have to do is multiply 5 x 5. Now suggest the first nine odd numbers (9 x 9). You will look like a total genius and they will never guess how you can add up so quickly!

Here are some shapes with a mirror line.
Draw the reflection that you would expect to see.

Warm-up

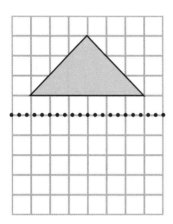

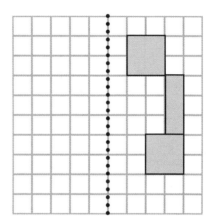

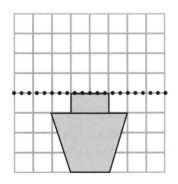

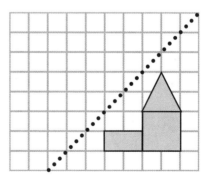

11 Magic square

Each number from 1 to 9 needs to be placed in the grid so that every line (horizontal, vertical and diagonal) adds up to 15.

	9	
	1	

I like l-o-n-g numbers so here is my favourite trick. Can you continue the pattern to make a number that is as long as my neck? You might need a calculator to help you.

$$1 \times 1 = 1$$
$$11 \times 11 = 121$$
$$111 \times 111 = 12321$$

Solve the clues to find the missing numbers.
Remember to check the **Number facts** on pages
5–8 for help. Use the notepad as a working out area.

- I am smaller than 150.
- I am a square number.
- I have two digits and both of them are even numbers.
- I am a cube number.

What number am I?

- I have three digits and all of them are odd numbers.
- My last two digits are single prime numbers.
- My digits all run in size order, smallest first.
- The digits added together make the number 9.

What number am I?

 **Puzzle Pointer**

 Notepad

Start with one of the facts that
limit the number of options. Write
down the possible options. Now
read the other facts. Cross out
numbers that do not fit until you
have only one option.

Warm-up

Starting at the snake's tail, answer each sum one by one. Then write the final answer in the box by the snake's head. Remember to check the **Number facts** on pages 5–8 for help.

$3 \times 4 = 12$

3 × 4

+

8 ÷ 2

−

4^2

9 × 8

+

÷ 3

+

6 × 5

÷ 9

+

=

5^2

14 Stable fees

Holly Bush Stables offers boarding services for horses. Look at the board below and use it to solve the questions.

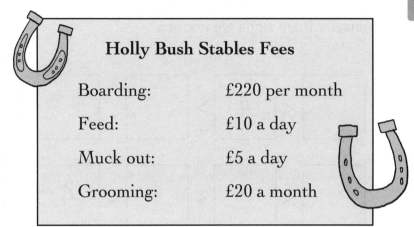

Holly Bush Stables Fees

Boarding: £220 per month

Feed: £10 a day

Muck out: £5 a day

Grooming: £20 a month

1. Lightning needs boarding, but no feed, for six months.

   How much is his bill?

2. Rubicon needs boarding and feed every day for July and August.

   How much is her bill?

3. Honey and Neddy need boarding, feed each day, mucking out and grooming for December.

   How much is their bill?

23

15 Futoshiki fun 1

Warm-up

Complete this Futoshiki board by making sure that the numbers 1, 2, 3 and 4 are placed on the board so that every vertical and horizontal line has one of each number in it and the > (greater than) and < (smaller than) signs are correct.

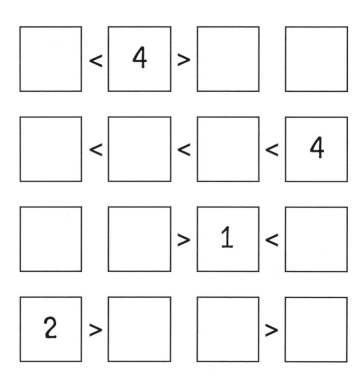

 **Puzzle Pointer**

Remember that the big part of the arrow is next to the bigger number and the small part of the arrow is next to the smaller number.

16 Cell crunching 1

In this puzzle, the three numbers in each horizontal row must add up to the number in the shaded grey box on the left. The three numbers in each vertical column must add up to the number in the shaded grey box at the top.

Put the numbers from the box in the right place.

1, 2, 4, 4, 6, 8, 8, 9, 9

The first two numbers have been done for you.

Puzzle Pointer

Cross off each number as you write it in the grid. This will make it easy to see what numbers you have left.

	23	7	21
14			
17		2	
20			8

25

17 Bull's eye 1

Ali is playing a darts game. He chooses a number to be the bull's eye and then throws four darts to see what numbers they land on. He can only use + and − and the four numbers in any order to reach his target. How does he do it? The first one has been done for you.

Bull's eye: 11

Darts: 4 8 9 6

Answer: $(6 + 9) - (8 - 4) = 11$

Bull's eye: 20

Darts: 12 13 2 3

Answer:

Bull's eye: 3

Darts: 11 5 7 10

Answer:

Look at the numbers. Can you work out what answers should be written above the two cats at the bottom of the page?

 Puzzle Pointer

Look at the two bottom numbers on the first two hats. What do you have to do to them to get the number at the top of the hat?

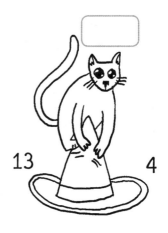

19 Silly sevens

Warm-up

> If I write down all the numbers from 1 to 100, how many times will I write down a 7?

How many sevens will Rose write down?

> I am going on holiday. To get there I have to travel through seven tunnels. At each tunnel, I have to pay a fee of $\frac{1}{2}$ of all the money that I have when I enter the tunnel. I need to arrive with £2.

How much money does Byron need to take with him to arrive with £2?

Notepad

20 Sudoku fun 1

Complete the grid by placing the numbers 1 to 9 on every row so that:

- Each row has only one of each number.
- Each column has only one of each number.
- Each block of nine squares has only one of each number.

Warm-up

	9	1	7	5	4	2	8	
2		7	3	6	1	4		9
6	5		2	9	8		3	1
5	4	8		2		1	9	7
7	2	9	1		5	6	4	3
1	6	3		4		8	2	5
4	3		5	1	2		7	8
8		5	4	7	9	3		2
	7	2	8	3	6	5	1	

29

21 Nine times table

Warm-up

The answers to these nine times tables questions fit into the grid. Write the answers in words.

Across

1.   2 × 9

7.   7 × 9

8.   1 × 9

Down

2.   3 × 9

3.   9 × 9

4.   8 × 9

5.   4 × 9

6.   5 × 9

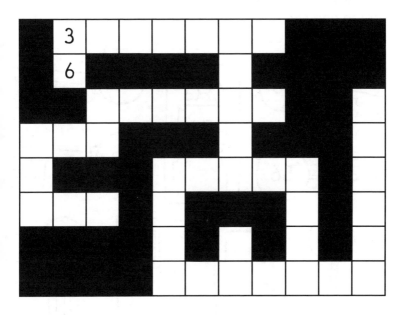

22 Fill the grid 1

Put all of the numbers below into the grid. The first one has been done for you.

36	365	1961
47	369	2345
99	512	

| 12345 | 258520 | 1478520 |
| 18562 | 976431 | 3579512 |

Warm-up

Here are ten keys and five doors. The keys and doors all have numbers. You are looking for a key that is $\frac{3}{4}$ of the number of a door. Draw a line to match each key to the right door. You will have some keys left over.

24 Number train 1

Follow the passengers carefully!

- The train leaves the station with 37 passengers.

- At the first stop 29 people get off and 112 people get on.

- At the second stop 53 people get off and 96 people get on.

- At the third stop 47 people get off and 153 people get on.

- The train reaches the final destination.

How many people are on the train? ☐

- When it returns the train has 182 passengers on it.

- At the first stop 18 people get off and 72 people get on.

- At the second stop 105 people get off and 81 people get on.

- At the third stop 96 people get off and 41 people get on.

- The train reaches the final destination.

How many people are on the train? ☐

Warm-up

(25) Break the safe

There is money in the safe but nobody can work out the code to get in. The code is written down in numbers but can only be inputted using letters.

Use the following information and solve the code for the safe.

You have just five minutes before the safe is permanently locked. Good luck!

$$7 \times 6 = D \qquad\qquad 32 \div 4 = E$$

$$12 \times 3 = L \qquad\qquad 15 \times 4 = N$$

$$132 \div 11 = O \qquad\qquad 27 \div 9 = W$$

| 3 | 8 | 36 | 36 | | 42 | 12 | 60 | 8 |

___ ___ ___ ___   ___ ___ ___ ___

Notepad

I have another puzzle for you. What three whole numbers have exactly the same answer when you add them together as when you multiply them together?

Instead of five ponds with four fish in each, there are four ponds with five fish. Work out the answer to each sum, then choose the odd one out from each pond that needs to be moved into the empty pond.

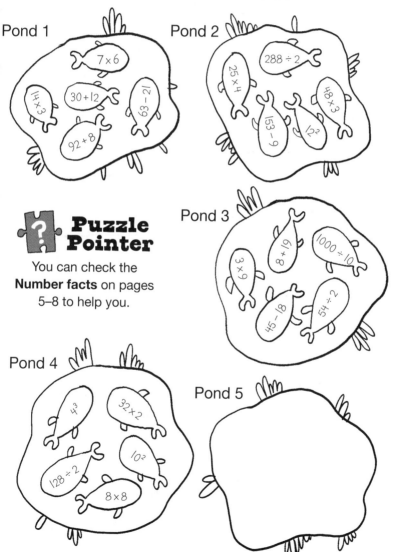

Pond 1

7×6
14×3
$30 + 12$
$63 - 21$
$92 + 8$

Pond 2

$288 \div 2$
25×4
$153 - 9$
12^2
48×3

Puzzle Pointer

You can check the **Number facts** on pages 5–8 to help you.

Pond 3

3×9
8×19
$1000 \div 10$
$45 - 18$
$54 \div 2$

Pond 4

4^3
32×2
10^2
$128 \div 2$
8×8

Pond 5

Warm-up

The café is selling four new maths sandwiches. To make a sandwich there is a number on the top, a number in the filling, in the salad and on the bottom. Each new number is found by following the recipe above each sandwich.

Divide by 2 each time.

Sandwich 1

Divide by 3 each time.

Sandwich 2

Add 17 each time.

Sandwich 3

Multiply by 5 each time.

Sandwich 4

Look at the grid below. Each symbol represents the number 1, 2 or 3. The total for each row is given at the beginning of the row in the grey box. The total for each column is given at the top of the column in the grey box.

Which number does each symbol represent?
The first one has been done for you.

	7	6	5
6	🚫	☆	❤
7	❤	❤	☆
5	🚫	🚫	☆

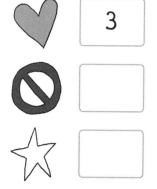

❤ = 3

🚫 =

☆ =

Puzzle Pointer

Look at the rows and columns with the smallest value. The final column has a score of 5, so the star cannot be worth 3. The bottom row has a score of 5, so the circular shape cannot be worth 3. The heart must be worth 3.

29 Number pyramids 1

Rachel and Marion make some number pyramids. Whatever Rachel does, Marion copies the same pattern.

In a number pyramid, the numbers on the lower levels determine the numbers above them. Fill in the missing numbers from Marion's pyramids.

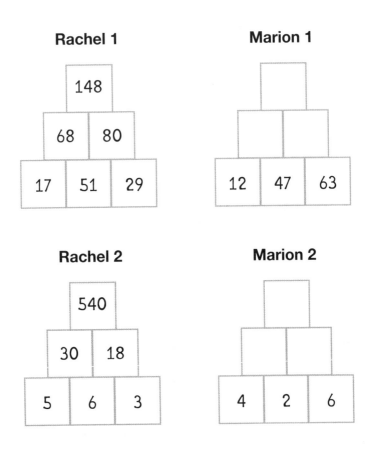

Rachel 1

148

68 | 80

17 | 51 | 29

Marion 1

12 | 47 | 63

Rachel 2

540

30 | 18

5 | 6 | 3

Marion 2

4 | 2 | 6

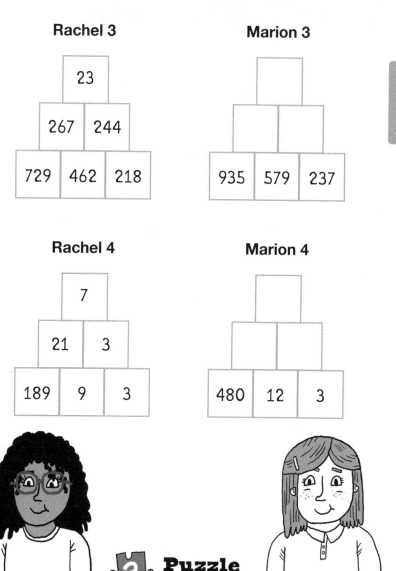

Rachel 3

	23	
267		244
729	462	218

Marion 3

935	579	237

Rachel 4

	7	
21		3
189	9	3

Marion 4

480	12	3

Puzzle Pointer

Look at the bottom two numbers and see how they have been used to make the number above them. Once you have found the pattern, use the same method to complete the other pyramid.

Warm-up

Warm-up

The number in the centre must be reached by adding all the numbers that are around the outside of the spinning top. Fill in the missing numbers.

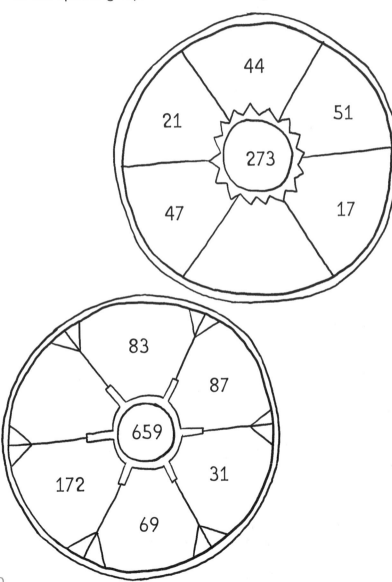

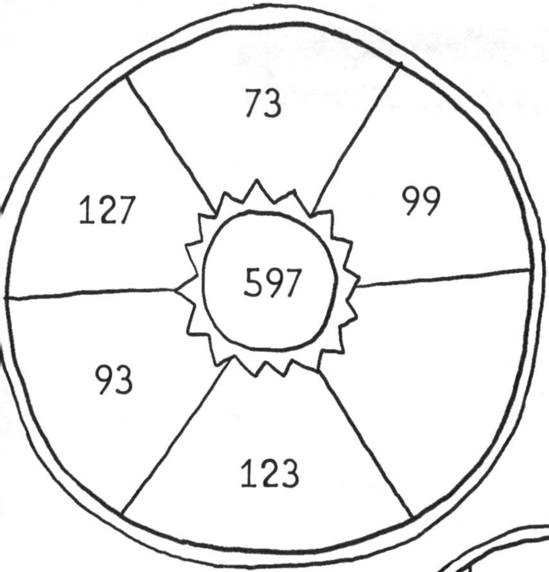

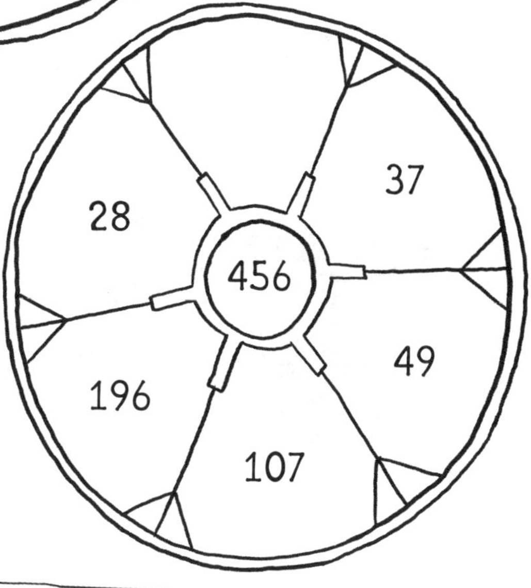

Wheel 1

- 73
- 99
- 127
- 597 (center)
- 93
- 123

Wheel 2

- 37
- 28
- 456 (center)
- 49
- 196
- 107

Notepad

Use the passports below to answer the questions about the bears.

Name: Snowy Bear

Date of Birth: 07.05.2015

Place of Birth: Lapland

12513687

Name: Brown Bear

Date of Birth: 25.06.2015

Place of Birth: Iceland

93461084

Name: Daisy Bear

Date of Birth: 29.02.2016

Place of Birth: Greenland

12513687

Name: Fred Bear

Date of Birth: 07.11.2014

Place of Birth: England

12513687

1. Which bear is the oldest?

   _____

2. Which bear is the youngest?

   _____

3. Which bear is a summer-born bear?

   _____

4. What is special about Daisy Bear's birthday?

   _____

5. Which two bears are exactly six months apart in age?

   _____

Puzzle Pointer

Remember that the smaller the
year, the older the bear.

Warm-up

Look at the grid map below and then plot the robot as it makes its way around. The first instruction (N3) has been done for you.

10										
9										
8										
7										
6										
5										
4										
3										
2										
1										
	A	B	C	D	E	F	G	H	I	J

North = N   South = S   East = E   West = W

I begin on A1 and move...

N3, E5, S1, W3, N3, E2, S5, E4, N8

Where do I end up? [   ]

Puzzle Pointer

N3 means move North 3 squares.
E5 means move East 5 squares and so on.

33 Number finder 1

Warm-up

Solve the number questions and then find your answers in the number grid. Your answers might be vertical, horizontal or diagonal. One has been done for you.

100 x 10 = _____   144 ÷ 12 = _____   432 + 59 = _____

57 x 10 = _____   450 ÷ 5 = _____   876 − 543 = _____

19 x 3 = _____   712 + 509 = _121_   753 − 246 = _____

512 ÷ 8 = _____   31 + 287 = _____   139 − 86 = _____

3	4	5	7	0	3	0	2
2	1	8	6	4	1	3	4
1	5	0	5	9	8	3	7
2	0	8	0	7	0	3	6
4	7	5	3	0	4	9	1
7	1	2	2	1	2	3	9

34 Bunny hop race

The bunny hop is the biggest race in the animal athletics. Each bunny jumps using their own unique bunny-hopping style. Fill in the missing numbers for each bunny.

I'm Honey Bunny and I have to jump forwards five jumps and backwards two jumps.

I'm Sunny Bunny and I have to jump forwards seven jumps and backwards five jumps.

I'm Funny Bunny and I have to jump forwards eight jumps and backwards four jumps.

46

Honey	Sunny	Funny
0	0	0
5	7	8
3	2	4

Which bunny wins the race? _____

(35) How many?

Alex is sewing pencil cases to sell at the school fair. He has a roll of fabric and knows how much he needs for each pencil case. Each pencil case needs:

50 centimetres of green fabric

20 centimetres of white fabric

15 centimetres of brown fabric

1 zip

Alex has:

12 metres of green fabric

5 metres of white fabric

3 metres of brown fabric

40 zips

How many complete pencil cases can Alex make?

Notepad

Puzzle Pointer

Alex might have 40 zips, but this doesn't mean he can make 40 pencil cases if he doesn't have enough fabric. Work out how many pencil cases Alex can make from the green fabric, the white fabric, the brown fabric and the zips.

(36) Funny fours

A and B are two sides of the same card. Which side of the card has more fours in it – A or B?

Card 1

A

224 344 747
314 444
435 742 844
564 434 974 924

B

444 413 794
814 514
245 844 434
314 634 479
431

Card 2

A

744 754 994
994 864
454 244 343
864 471
475 114

B

104 444 749
314 124
644 284 974
814 344
374 154

Card 3

A

544 334 114
144 424
474 734 944
374 734 494
473

B

448 314 474
344 814
343 744 414
344 434
114 144

37 Hot-air balloons

Warm-up

Sally and Mikkel are at a hot-air balloon show.
Of the 36 hot-air balloons they can see floating by:

- $\frac{1}{12}$ have vertical stripes

- 25% have wavy lines

- $\frac{1}{6}$ have a dotted pattern

- $\frac{1}{3}$ are plain white and the rest have horizontal stripes.

Decorate the hot-air balloons to show what they can see.

51

Puzzle power!

How did you do? Do you have puzzle power? Check the answers at the end of the book and add up how many warm-up puzzles you got right. Score 2 for each fully correct puzzle, and 1 if you got some of the puzzle right. Then write down your total and read on to discover your puzzle power ...

My puzzle power score is

Puzzle power score 0–25

Great start! Your puzzle power has begun to grow. Why don't you go over some of the puzzles you weren't sure about before going on to the next puzzles?

Puzzle power score 26–49

Well done! Your puzzle power is growing and you're getting warmed up for the intermediate puzzles.

Puzzle power score 50+

Wow, you have dazzling puzzle power! You are ready to zoom straight to the intermediate puzzles and take on some more puzzle challenges.

Intermediate puzzles

38 Monkey maze

Four monkeys are trying to reach the bananas by swinging through the numbered squares. They can only swing to a number that is above, below, to the right or to the left of the square they are on.

- Monkey A has to use the numbered squares in the three times table.

- Monkey B has to use the numbered squares in the five times table.

- Monkey C has to use the numbered squares that are in the six times table.

- Monkey D has to use the numbered squares that are in the seven times table.

Only one monkey can reach the bananas.

Which monkey is it?

Intermediate

A Start ↓   B Start ↓

12	**3**	13	15	56	55	60	45	**5**	9
33	9	18	80	65	40	29	38	15	19
15	24	27	6	30	79	80	46	35	29
2	87	40	34	31	51	62	72	20	75
16	28	31	26	29	37	52	62	47	95
34	19	20					12	52	80
10	14	35					29	36	61
52	70	13					14	31	92
69	56	51	68	57	46	26	19	71	86
9	35	84	77	49	14	17	23	31	24
12	21	11	81	30	42	35	67	19	13
36	26	39	46	12	43	21	31	46	4
18	**6**	24	60	72	29	63	28	**7**	15

C Start ↑   D Start ↑

Solve these monster maths problems.

 = 39

 = 41

 = 27

 =

 =

Intermediate

40 Fifty point break

All of the balls have a number on them. Draw a line to join two balls together so that they add up to 50. Which ball does not have a partner?

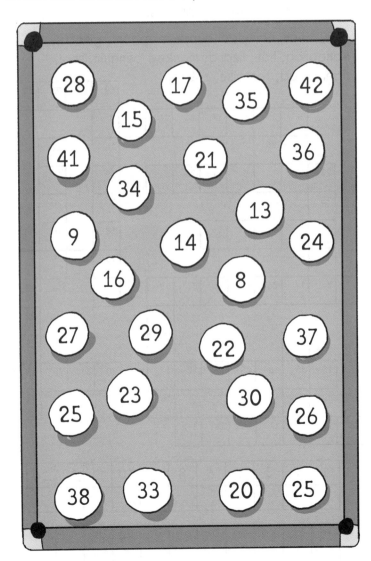

57

41 Zoo link words

Each letter has a number code assigned to it. Two letters have been filled in for you. Solve the letter and number code to turn the number grid into the names of these animals:

ape, bear, camel, cheetah, elephant, giraffe, kangaroo, lion, lizard, monkey, penguin, seal, tiger, toad, tortoise, zebra

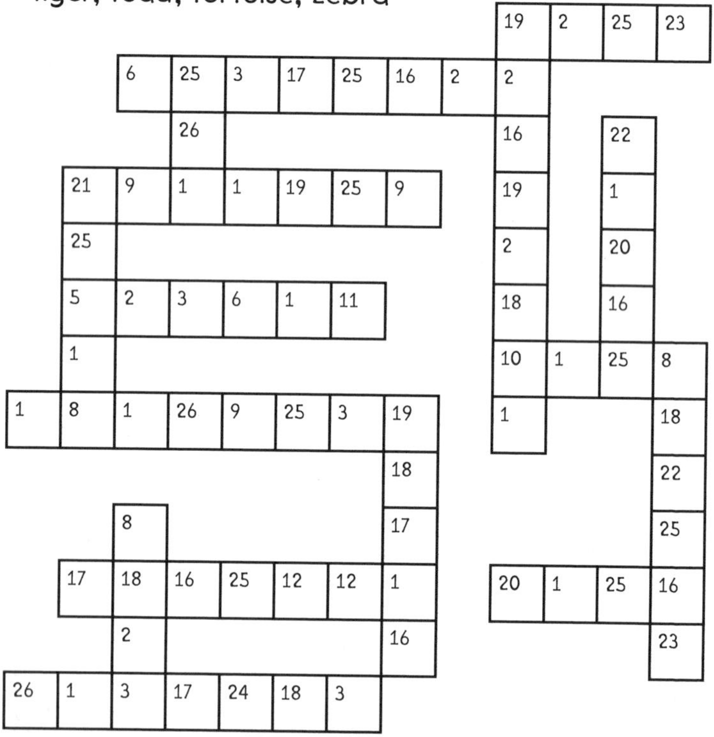
19 2 25 23
6 25 3 17 25 16 2 2
26 16 22
21 9 1 1 19 25 9 19 1
25 2 20
5 2 3 6 1 11 18 16
1 10 1 25 8
1 8 1 26 9 25 3 19 1 18
18 22
8 17 25
17 18 16 25 12 12 1 20 1 25 16
2 16 23
26 1 3 17 24 18 3

1	2	3	5	6	8	9	10	11	12	16
E										

17	18	19	20	21	22	23	24	25	26
		T							

Draw lines to connect shapes, making sure that the total number of sides adds up to 14.

- No line can touch another.

- You can only draw lines that are horizontal or vertical, not diagonal.

- You can join as many shapes together as you want.

One has been done for you.

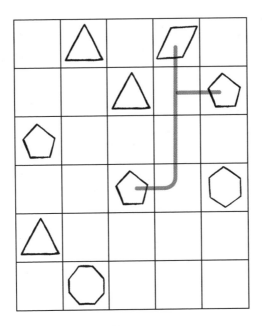

Puzzle Pointer

This puzzle can be answered in different ways.

The builders need to climb the ladders to reach the top of the house. Start at the bottom and complete the sums to climb up the ladders. Write the final number for each ladder in the top boxes.

Ladder 1:
× 2
× 5
+ 5^2
÷ 10
1000

Ladder 2:
× 4
÷ 3
+ 52
× 4
32

Ladder 3:
÷ 6
+ 48
× 3
− 8
40

These look like normal sentences but they are not!
Hidden between words or inside words are some
numbers. Draw a line under the numbers you find.
The first one has been done for you.

1. Who would no**t wo**nder why it was
   snowing in summer?

2. That chair has the comfort you need.

3. The little mouse ate nervously, always watchful.

4. I left the paper in the loft and it went yellow.

5. I reached the hotel eventually, tired and hungry.

6. The secretaries even typed the letter for me.

My name is Leo. My mother
Sarah had four children before
me: Maurice, Norris, Horace and
Boris. What is the name of her
youngest son?

(45) Cross out

Cross out one pair of numbers for each of these problems. You can only use each number once.

- A pair that add up to a square number.

- A pair that add up to a prime number.

- A pair that add up to the product of 3 and 5.

- A pair that add up to 100.

31   26

     37   4   3

62   58

     23   18

42   12

     14   29

Puzzle Pointer

There may be more than one answer to each question. Don't forget to check the **Number facts** on pages 5–8 if you need help remembering prime numbers or square numbers.

46 Shade art 2

Shade in the following numbers to reveal another number.

- Shade in all odd numbers under 50.
- Shade in all square numbers.
- Shade in the first ten triangular numbers.

2	48	12	44	14	40	8	32	53	42
46	30	34	20	26	24	38	51	22	50
38	31	10	25	16	4	48	15	46	2
12	1	26	18	81	29	22	16	26	51
44	24	14	28	6	8	50	3	54	30
34	8	36	45	2	44	14	25	12	34
22	29	21	32	40	20	38	4	50	22
30	4	81	29	10	36	32	31	2	48
48	12	42	26	44	50	18	42	52	24
14	38	20	34	8	46	24	40	30	18

 **Puzzle Pointer**

You can check the **Number facts** on pages 5–8 if you need help remembering square numbers or triangular numbers.

Here are some shapes with a mirror line.
Draw the reflection that you would expect to see.

Intermediate

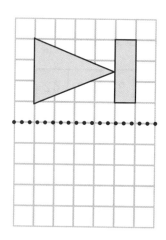

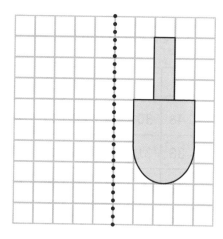

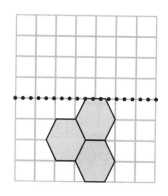

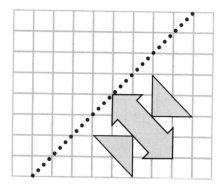

48 Number riddles 2

Solve the clues to find the missing numbers.

- I am larger than 100 but smaller than 200.

- I am a square number.

- I have three digits and two of them are odd numbers.

- My digits are in order of size.

- If I rearrange my last two numbers, and keep my first number where it is, I make another three-digit square number.

What number am I? ____

- I have three digits and all of them are different even numbers.

- If I multiply my first two digits, I make the third digit.

- My digits are in order of size.

- My second digit is a square number.

What number am I? ____

Puzzle Pointer

You could use the **Number facts** on pages 5–8 to remind you about square numbers.

Starting at the snake's tail, answer each sum one by one. Then write the final answer in the last box by the snake's head. Remember to check the **Number facts** on pages 5–8 for help.

Intermediate

$8 \times 7 = 56$

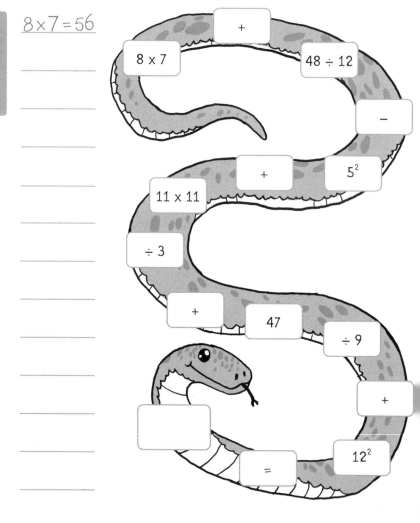

50 Sandcastles 2

In a number pyramid, the numbers on the lower levels determine the numbers on the line above them. Follow the pattern to fill in the missing numbers on the sandcastle.

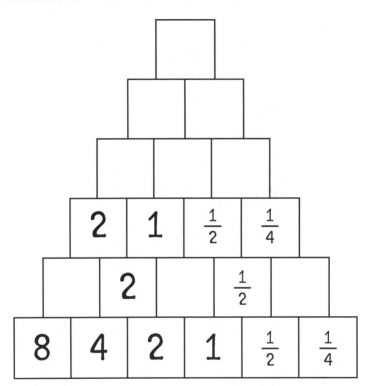

		2	1	$\frac{1}{2}$	$\frac{1}{4}$		
		2		$\frac{1}{2}$			
8	4	2	1	$\frac{1}{2}$	$\frac{1}{4}$		

Puzzle Pointer

Find the difference between each number on the bottom line and the number to the right of it to work out the numbers on the line above.

51 Grabber machine

Zara and Charlie have collected a few items from the grabber machine.

Circle the name of the child who has the more expensive collection of goodies.

£1.00

£1.50

£3.00   £2.00

Intermediate

Zara

Charlie

Complete this Futoshiki board. The numbers 1, 2, 3 and 4 are placed on the board so that every vertical and horizontal line has one of each number in it and the > (greater than) and < (smaller than) signs are correct.

Intermediate

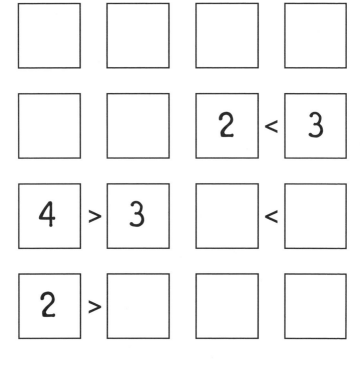

 Puzzle Pointer

You don't have to start at the top.
Find a line that's easy to fill in.

53 Cell crunching 2

In this puzzle, the three numbers in each horizontal row must add up to the number in the shaded grey box on the left. The three numbers in each vertical column must add up to the number in the shaded grey box at the top.

You can only have one of each number in the vertical columns and horizontal rows.

Put the numbers from the box in the right place.

1, 2, 2, 3, 4, 6, 7, 8, 9

The first number has been done for you.

	6	16	20
20	3		
15			
7			

54 Bull's eye 2

Ali is playing a darts game. He chooses a number to be the bull's eye and then throws four darts to see what numbers they land on. He can only use +, x, – and ÷ and the four numbers in any order to reach his target. How does he do it? The first one has been done for you.

Bull's eye: 33

Darts: 9   6   7   9

Answer: $(9 \times 9) - (7 \times 6) = 39$

Bull's eye: 450

Darts: 12   3   2   15

Answer:

Bull's eye: 60

Darts: 11   4   9   12

Answer:

55 Cats on hats 2

Look at the numbers and work out what answer should be written above the cat on the third hat. There are two steps to reach the answer.

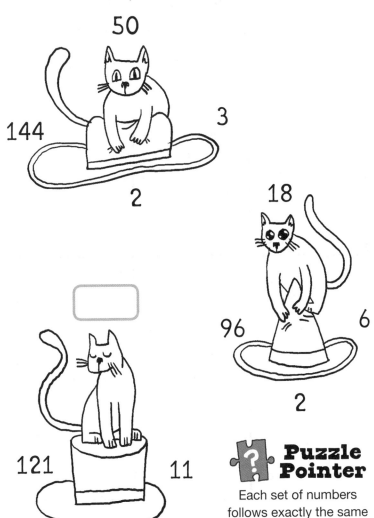

50

144   3

2

18

96   6

2

121   11

2

Puzzle Pointer

Each set of numbers follows exactly the same two-step sum.

Complete the grid by placing the numbers 1 to 9 on every row so that:

- Each row has only one of each number.

- Each column has only one of each number.

- Each block of nine squares has only one of each number.

Intermediate

6	1			4		8		5
	5		3	9		2	6	
4	3	2	8		6	7	9	
5	2	6	9		3	4		7
8	9	4		2		3	1	6
1	7		6	8				
2		1	4	6	5		7	3
9	4	7	1	3				2
		5		7	9	1	4	8

74

57 Fill the grid 2

Put all of the numbers below into the grid.
The first one has been done for you.

42	325	1357
59	679	1928
91	673	

| 15891 | 579310 | 7926831 |
| 40168 | 746551 | 9753246 |

Join groups of numbers together that make up a total of 25. You can have as many numbers in the group as you want and the numbers can be horizontal, vertical or diagonal. One group has been done for you.

Intermediate

9	7	8	7	5	5	1	2	2	4
9	4	5	5	3	5	1	5	3	4
1	3	3	3	4	5	9	8	6	3
2	4	2	6	5	5	5	7	6	6
4	5	1	2	1	6	7	1	1	6
6	8	1	2	1	2	1	9	3	1
4	3	3	5	1	5	6	5	6	2
4	5	4	4	4	4	4	4	1	6
5	7	6	6	1	4	3	4	1	5
9	5	5	2	7	6	5	2	3	4

Puzzle Pointer

If you join all the possible groups of numbers that make 25, there will be no spare numbers on the grid.

Here are ten keys and five doors. The keys and doors all have numbers. You are looking for a key that has the same value as a door. Draw a line to match each key to the right door. You will have some keys left over.

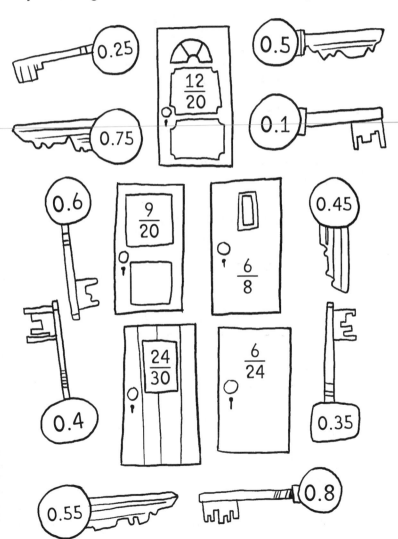

Intermediate

Follow the passengers carefully!

- The train leaves the station with 149 passengers on it.

- At the first stop 71 people get off and 162 people get on.

- At the second stop 53 people get off and 239 people get on.

- At the third stop 57 people get off and 314 people get on.

- The train reaches the final destination.

How many people are on the train?

- To return the train has 437 passengers on it.

- At the first stop 218 people get off and 112 people get on.

- At the second stop 196 people get off and 68 people get on.

- At the third stop 85 people get off and 96 people get on.

- The train reaches the final destination.

How many people are on the train?

Intermediate

61 Fishy business 2

Instead of five ponds with four fish in each, there are four ponds with five fish. Work out the answer to each sum, then choose the odd one out from each pond that needs to be moved into the empty pond.

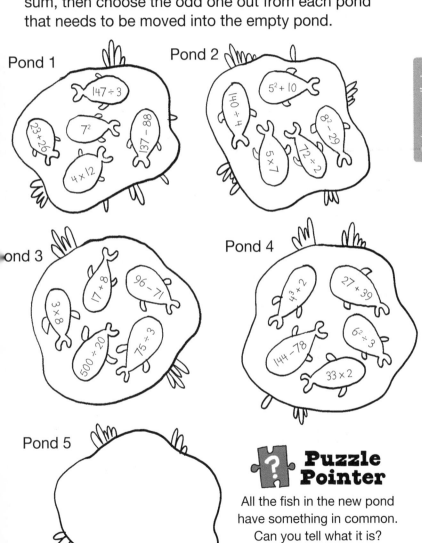

Pond 1

$147 \div 3$

7^2

$23 + 26$

$137 - 88$

4×12

Pond 2

$5^2 + 10$

$140 \div 4$

5×7

$7^2 \div 2$

$8^2 - 29$

Pond 3

$17 + 8$

$96 - 71$

3×8

$500 \div 20$

$75 \div 3$

Pond 4

$4^3 + 2$

$27 + 39$

$144 - 78$

$6^2 \div 3$

33×2

Pond 5

Puzzle Pointer

All the fish in the new pond have something in common. Can you tell what it is?

Intermediate

79

Five cats have been accused of pinching a basket full of fish.

Use the following information and solve the code to find out who it was.

56 ÷ 8 =	H	10 x 7 =	N	11 x 1 =	R
2 x 12 =	C	12 ÷ 6 =	F	48 ÷ 8 =	I
8 x 9 =	G	24 ÷ 8 =	T	5 x 8 =	A
45 ÷ 9 =	O	6 x 5 =	M	81 ÷ 81 =	L
3 x 9 =	U	12 x 4 =	S	64 ÷ 16 =	Y
4 x 13 =	E	27 ÷ 3 =	D	2 x 4 =	V

6, 48 / 6, 3 /
7, 27, 70, 72, 11, 4 /
7, 5, 11, 40, 24, 52?

_____

_____

6, 48   6, 3
2, 40, 30, 6, 48, 7, 52, 9
2, 1, 27, 2, 2, 4?

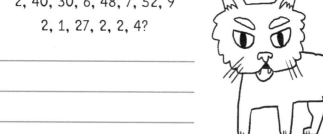

_____

_____

_____

80

6, 48 / 6, 3 /
48, 3, 40, 11, 8, 6, 70, 72 /
48, 5, 5, 3, 4?

_____

_____

_____

6, 48 / 6, 3 /
72, 11, 52, 52, 9, 4 /
72, 6, 72, 6?

_____

_____

_____

6, 48 / 6, 3 /
11, 40, 8, 52, 70, 5, 27, 48 /
11, 40, 72, 3, 40, 6, 1?

_____

_____

_____

3, 7, 52 / 72, 27, 6, 1, 3, 4 / 24, 40, 3 /
6, 48 / 2, 40, 30, 6, 48, 52, 9 / 2, 1, 27, 2, 2, 4

_____

_____

_____

63 Maths sandwiches 2

The café is selling four new maths sandwiches. To make a sandwich there is a number on the top, a number in the filling, in the salad and on the bottom. Each new number is found by following the recipe above each sandwich.

Divide by 4 each time.

Sandwich 1

320

Subtract 117 each time.

Sandwich 2

597

Multiply by 2 each time.

Sandwich 3

543

Multiply by $1\frac{1}{2}$ each time.

Sandwich 4

800

64 Symbolic sums 2

Look at the grid below. Each symbol represents one number: 1, 2, 3 or 4. The total for each row is given at the beginning of the row in the grey box. The total for each column is given at the top of the column in the grey box.

Which number does each symbol represent?

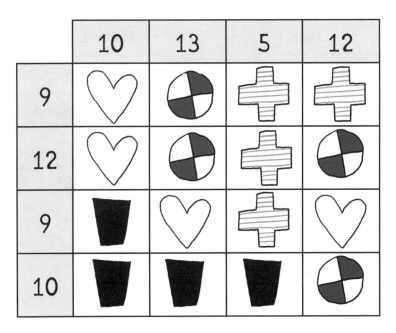

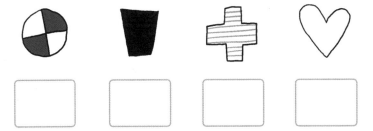

83

Jack and Harry make some number pyramids.
Whatever Jack does, Harry copies the same pattern.

In a number pyramid, the numbers on the lower
levels determine the numbers above them. Fill in the
missing numbers from Harry's pyramids. The first one
has been done for you.

Intermediate

Jack 1   **Harry 1**

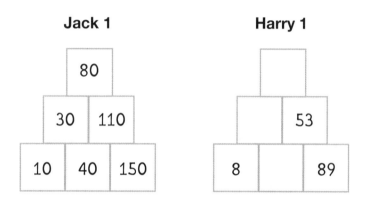

Jack 2   **Harry 2**

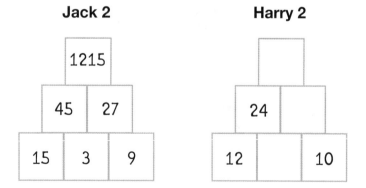

84

Solve the number questions and then find your answers in the number grid. Your answers might be vertical or horizontal and they cannot overlap. The first one has been done for you. Look at the **Number facts** on pages 5–8 if you need help working out the cubed number.

47 × 3 = _141_	136 + 249 = _____
27 × 4 = _____	987 + 132 = _____
560 ÷ 8 = _____	23 × 6 = _____
169 ÷ 13 = _____	963 – 246 = _____
5^3 = _____	29 × 10 = _____
15 × 5 = _____	846 ÷ 3 = _____

7	1	7	7	6	2	9	3
1	3	6	5	3	9	1	8
9	8	1	4	1	0	0	5
1	1	1	9	5	1	8	6
3	7	2	8	2	2	9	4
2	0	1	3	8	5	0	5

(67) Spinning tops 2

The number in the centre must be reached by adding all the numbers that are around the outside of the spinning top. Fill in the missing numbers.

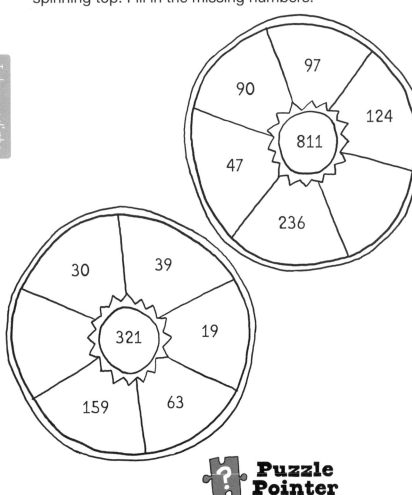

Puzzle Pointer

Using columns, line up the decimal points of the numbers you're adding. Add the numbers in the same way you would add three-digit numbers.

Wheel 1: centre 5, with segments: 10, -9, -12, 15, 8

Wheel 2: centre 2, with segments: 0.1, 0.03, 0.04, 0.5, 0.4

Notepad

68 Gridlock 1

The grid is locked until the correct numbers are put in the right place. Put the following numbers into the grid so that each number statement is correct.

$$1 \quad 2 \quad 4 \quad 6$$

- The number statements must be correct both vertically and horizontally.
- Each number can only be used once.

	+		=	10
+	■	−	■	÷
	×		=	2
=	■	=	■	=
8	−	3	=	5

If 14 cats had each caught two rats, and upon each rat was a six-legged gnat, how many legs were there altogether?

88

Look at the grid map below and then plot the robot's path as it makes its way around. The first move (N8) has been done for you.

10										
9										
8										
7										
6										
5										
4										
3										
2										
1										
	A	B	C	D	E	F	G	H	I	J

North = N   South = S   East = E   West = W

Intermediate

I begin on A1 and move...

N8, E3, S4, W1, S3, E3, N8, E3, S3, W1, S2, E1, S2, W1, S2, E2

Where do I end up?

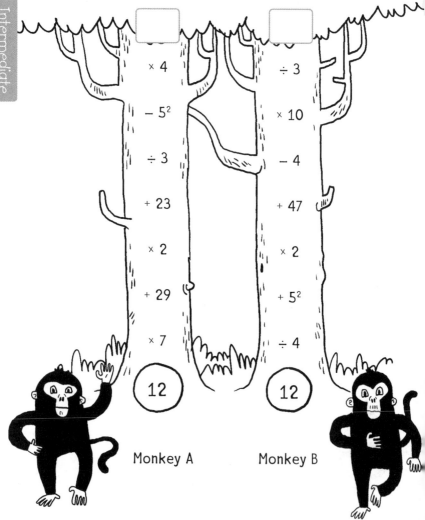

Two monkeys are climbing the trees. Follow the maths instructions to find out which monkey reaches the top of the tree with the highest score. Remember to use the **Number facts** on pages 5–8 if you need help working out the square numbers.

Intermediate

Monkey A

× 4

− 5²

÷ 3

+ 23

× 2

+ 29

× 7

12

Monkey B

÷ 3

× 10

− 4

+ 47

× 2

+ 5²

÷ 4

12

Blocks 1

Pavith and Kareen are playing the blocks game on their computers. The final scores have been revealed. Work out who has won the game using the scoring system below.

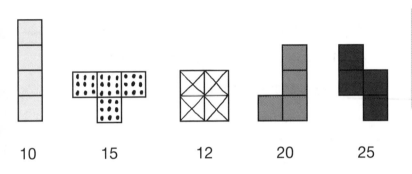

| 10 | 15 | 12 | 20 | 25 |

Intermediate

Pavith's screen

Kareen's screen

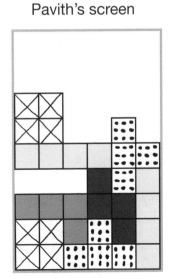 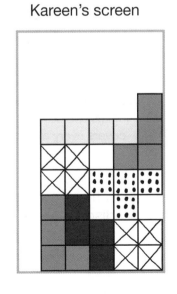

Intermediate

Lizzy, Ashley and Madison are sewing mobile phone covers to sell at the school fair.

Use the information below to solve the problems.

- Lizzy can make two covers in an hour.

- Ashley can make three covers in an hour.

- Madison can make four covers in an hour.

- They begin sewing at the same time.

- They sew from 9 a.m. until 4 p.m.

- They have a lunch break of 60 minutes, which they take at the same time.

 **Puzzle Pointer**

Work out how many hours they are sewing for. Then for each child multiply the number of hours by the number of covers they make. Work out what time each child completes a cover, e.g. Lizzie makes two covers an hour so she completes covers every o'clock and half past the hour.

1. How many covers do Lizzy, Ashley and Madison make in total?

2. How many times do all of them complete a cover at the same time?

3. How many times do Lizzy and Ashley finish a cover at the same time?

4. How many times do Lizzy and Madison finish a cover at the same time?

Notepad

To stop the reindeer feeling cold in the winter, they decide to put on some antler covers.

Decorate the reindeer so that:

- $\frac{1}{3}$ have horizontal stripes
- 10% have vertical stripes
- $\frac{1}{6}$ have a dotted pattern
- 1 in every 5 have a criss-crossed pattern
- 20% are plain white.

Intermediate

Puzzle Pointer

Work out the answer to each question first and then make sure your numbers add up to 30.

Puzzle power!

Is your puzzle power building as you do more puzzles? Check the answers at the end of the book and add up how many intermediate puzzles you got right. Score 2 for each fully correct puzzle, and 1 if you got some of the puzzle right. Then write down your total and read on to discover your puzzle power ...

My puzzle power score is _____ .

Puzzle power score 1–25

You like to take your time with things and have just dipped your toe in the puzzles. Look back over some of the puzzles before diving into the next ones.

Puzzle power score 26–49

You're splashing about and having fun with the puzzles. As your confidence grows, so does your puzzle power. Keep it up.

Puzzle power score 50+

You're zipping through with lightning speed and your puzzle power is electrifying. You are ready to take on some tricky puzzle challenges.

Tricky
puzzles

Solve these monster maths problems.

 = 7

 = 42

 = 64

 =

 =

Tricky

 **Puzzle Pointer**

Begin with the third line. Then look at which numbers could complete the second line and try these numbers in the first line.

Swinging on a star

Move from the top to the bottom of the page by linking stars that have numbers from the same times table.

- You can't use the one or two times tables.
- You must use the same times table each time.
- Beware as some stars lead to a dead end.
- You can't cross over the grey – you can only move to a star that is touching another.

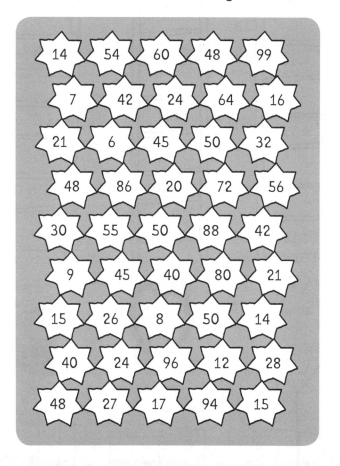

Tricky

99

76 Number ladders 3

The sailors need to climb the ladders to reach the top of their sails. Start at the bottom and complete the sums to climb up the ladders. Write the final number for each ladder in the top boxes.

Ladder 1 (bottom to top):
512
÷ 64
× 0.5
÷ 10
× 3

Ladder 2 (bottom to top):
63
− 100
× 2
+ 50
× 0.25

Ladder 3 (bottom to top):
0
+ 0.75
× 5
÷ 3
− 1.25

Tricky

100

Open the box 2

Complete the next two numbers in these sequences.
Then follow the instructions to find your key.

Puzzle Pointer

Remember to use the **Number facts**
on pages 5–8 to help you.

1.   186   157   128   99   70   ☐ ☐

2.   173   146   119   92   65   ☐ ☐

3.   1   2   3   5   8   13   21   ☐ ☐

4.   103   93   94   84   85   ☐ ☐

5.   512   343   216   125   64   ☐ ☐

6. Now add up your answers to make
   a three-digit number and write it here: ☐

7. Add up the three digits
   and write the number here: ☐

If the number is a triangular number, circle Key A.

If the number is not a triangular number, circle Key B.

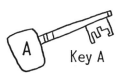

Key A

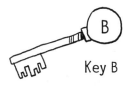

Key B

Tricky

Nish makes a number greater than 4 but less than 6. He can only use the numbers 4 and 6.

What is the number Nish makes?

Jasmine is making up party bags for her birthday guests. She has:

- hats in three different colours: gold, silver and pink

- four different types of gift: a sticky lizard, a glitter gel pen, a sheet of stickers and a mini slinky

- five different types of mini birthday cake: chocolate, lemon, vanilla, fruit and jam.

Can Jasmine make up 45 party bags so that every bag is different?

 **Puzzle Pointer**

The trick is to multiply the numbers together to get the total number of possible combinations.

Can you work out how old I am?

- I first laid eggs on my 25th birthday year and I have laid eggs every five years since.
- I have laid eggs 14 times.
- I will lay more eggs next year.

How old is the tortoise?

Zara has thought of a number. Can you work out what it is from these clues?

- Tom guessed 41.
- Ling guessed 47.
- Anuj guessed 53.
- Fred guessed 61.
- Amelie guessed 68.

Tricky

One person was 2 away, one was 4 away, one was 8 away, one was 12 away and one was 19 away.

What was the number Zara thought of?

 **Puzzle Pointer**

Write down the possible numbers that are 2 away from each of the children's guesses. Then cross off the numbers in your list that are not also 4 away from each of the guesses. Then cross off the numbers that are not also 8 away and so on until there is only 1 possible answer.

Shade in the following numbers to reveal another number.

- Shade in all prime numbers.
- Shade in all square numbers.
- Shade in all cube numbers.

1	4	29	9	64	16	23	8
49	10	25	15	52	86	20	64
64	15	31	48	100	27	60	19
27	6	81	14	4	8	42	11
81	24	9	26	54	68	56	23
3	20	2	49	125	16	28	17
8	52	25	16	19	7	14	81
36	38	8	5	1	49	40	8
7	30	27	7	3	25	6	29
64	5	25	8	2	11	37	13

 Puzzle Pointer

Look at the **Number facts** on pages 5–8 if you need help identifying the prime numbers, square numbers or cube numbers.

80 Mirror butterfly

Draw the reflection in the mirror line.

 **Puzzle Pointer**

You might find it easiest to start drawing the butterfly's body. Then draw the inside of the wings and work your way towards the outside.

? Try this riddle: ?

What number am I? I am an odd number but if you take away one letter from my name I become even.

Tricky

Solve the clues to find the missing numbers.

- I am larger than 500 but smaller than 1000.

- I have 3 digits and each of them is an even number.

- My digits are different and in reverse size order.

- The total of my three digits adds up to 18.

What number am I?

Tricky

- I have five digits and they make the same number forwards and backwards.

- All of my digits are prime numbers.

- My first three digits are in size order smallest to largest.

- The range of my numbers is three.

What number am I?

Notepad

 Puzzle Pointer

Look at the clues and work out the possible numbers then cross out the numbers that don't fit with the remaining clues.

(82) Snake sum 3

Starting at the snake's tail, answer each sum one by
one. Then write the final answer in the last box by the
snake's head. Remember to check the **Number facts**
on pages 5–8 for help.

$15 \times 4 = 60$

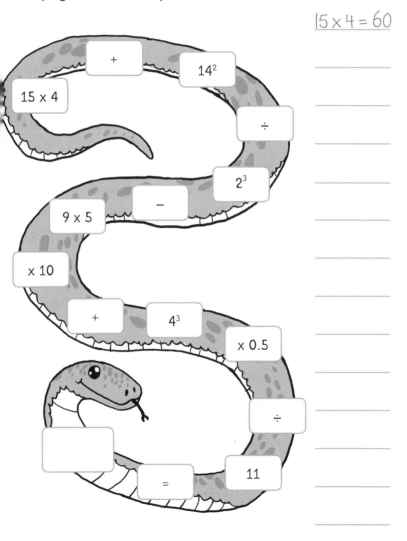

83 Shape-shifter

Work out what each shape is worth using the sums.

$$\square + \square + \square + \bigcirc = 25$$

$$\bigcirc + \bigcirc + \bigcirc + \square = 35$$

$$\square = \boxed{}$$

$$\bigcirc = \boxed{}$$

Puzzle Pointer

If you add the two answers together what is the answer? Now divide this by eight – what do you have? This will be the middle point between the value of the two shapes.

In a number pyramid, the numbers on the lower levels determine the numbers above them. Follow the pattern to fill in the sandcastle.

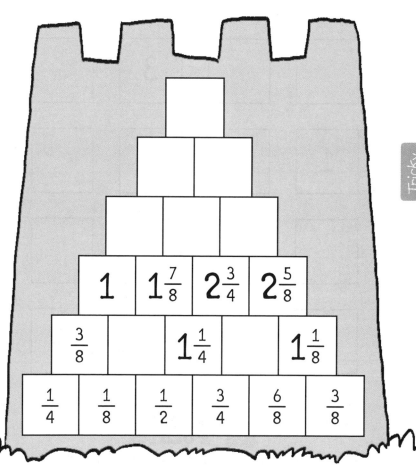

Tricky

Complete this Futoshiki board. The numbers 1, 2, 3 and 4 must be placed on the board so that every vertical and horizontal line has one of each number in it and the > (greater than) and < (smaller than) signs are correct.

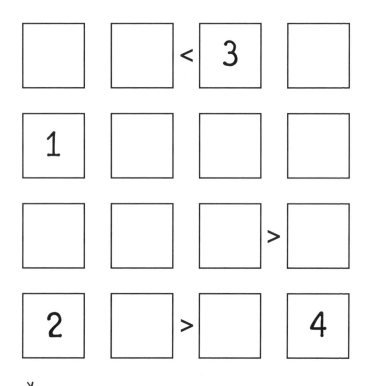

Puzzle Pointer

Look carefully at where the greater than and smaller than signs are and lightly fill in the possible numbers so you can change any answer easily if you need to.

In this puzzle, the three numbers in each horizontal row must add up to the number in the shaded grey box on the left. The three numbers in each vertical column must add up to the number in the shaded grey box at the top.

You can only have one of each number in the vertical columns and horizontal rows.

Put the numbers from the box in the right place.

6, 8, 8, 9, 12, 14, ~~15~~, 29, 31

The first number has been done for you.

Tricky

	32	43	57
75	15		
31			
26			

87 Bull's eye 3

Ali is playing a darts game. He chooses a number to be the bull's eye and then throws four darts to see what numbers they land on. He can only use +, x, – and ÷ and the four numbers in any order to reach his target. How does he do it? The first one has been done for you.

Bull's eye: 40

Darts: 3   8   4   7

Answer: (7 + 3) x (8 – 4) = 40

Tricky

Bull's eye: 74

Darts: 15   8   5   9

Answer:

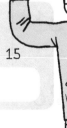

Bull's eye: 24

Darts: 11   13   15   15

Answer:

112

Look at the numbers and work out what answer should be written above the cat on the third hat. There are two steps to reach the answer.

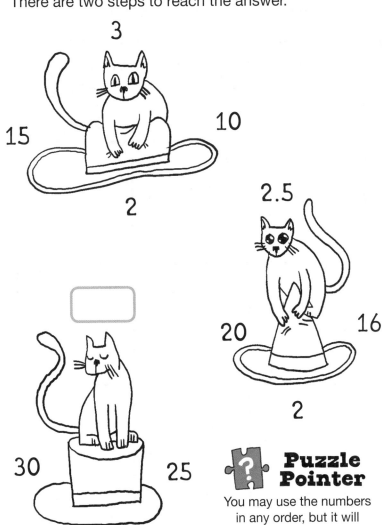

3

15

10

2

2.5

20

16

2

30

25

2

Puzzle Pointer

You may use the numbers in any order, but it will always be the same in each sum.

Tricky

89 Sudoku fun 3

Complete the grid by placing the numbers 1 to 9 on every row so that:

- Each row has only one of each number.
- Each column has only one of each number.
- Each block of nine squares has only one of each number.

	2	5	3		6		1	4
8	4		1	2	9		5	6
9		1	5				8	2
4	3			5	1	8	6	7
1		2		6	8			
	5	8		9	3	2	4	1
	9	6	8		7		2	
3		7	6		2	4		5
2	1		9		5		7	

90 Mixed times tables

The answers to these times tables questions fit into the grid. Write the answers in words.

Across

1. $560 \div 20$
3. 1.2×10
4. $4500 \div 900$
7. $8000 \div 2000$
8. 0.4×90
9. $900 \div 60$
10. 4×18

Down

1. 5^2
2. 3×9
5. 9^2
6. $640 \div 40$
7. $450 \div 10$

Tricky

Put the numbers below into the grid. The first one
has been done for you.

3
6
1

23   24   50   54   58   60   65   78   88   94

173   361   542   629   637   733   741   848   937   951

3344   5349

42360   83675

129856   807241

2838382   4261369

13572468

Tricky

Puzzle Pointer

Don't guess! The numbers either
run left to right **or** top to bottom
and can be solved logically. Put
the largest number in first and
then see what other numbers
can fit around it.

Here are ten keys and five doors. The keys and doors all have numbers. You are looking for a key that has **half** the value of a door. Draw a line to match each key to the right door. You will have some keys left over.

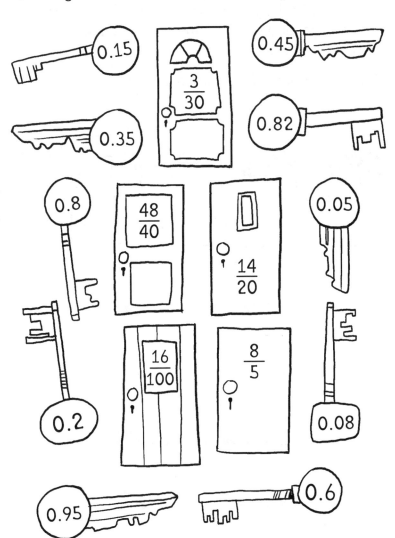

Tricky

117

(93) Products and sums

Some animals are given a number card with a single digit on it. Each number is different. They find a partner and work out the product and the sum of their numbers before they find another partner and do the same thing. They sometimes find more than one partner and work out the products and sums of their numbers.

Which number did each animal have?

Tricky

Hedgehog and Badger

Product = 45   Sum = 14

Tortoise and Giraffe

Product = 18   Sum = 9

Elephant, Hedgehog and Tortoise

Product = 60   Sum = 12

Tortoise, Badger and Elephant

Product = 108   Sum = 16

Hedgehog	
Badger	
Tortoise	
Giraffe	
Elephant	

 **Puzzle Pointer**

The product is the answer when two or more numbers are multiplied together. The sum is the answer when two or more numbers are added together.

Notepad

The finalists of the Animal of the Year contest have received their scoring cards. The animal with the most points wins.

Which animal wins the contest?

Round 1: Most intelligent animal

Badger	23.9
Elephant	34.6
Giraffe	19.0
Hedgehog	17.2
Lion	35.4
Tortoise	15.8

Round 2: Best personality

Badger	18.8
Elephant	16.5
Giraffe	19.1
Hedgehog	24.0
Lion	21.7
Tortoise	30.2

Notepad

Tricky

Round 3: Cutest looking animal

Badger	36.9
Elephant	32.8
Giraffe	31.6
Hedgehog	37.5
Lion	13.0
Tortoise	38.9

Round 4: Most talented animal

Badger	11.1
Elephant	23.3
Giraffe	21.1
Hedgehog	25.2
Lion	28.3
Tortoise	24.0

Now complete the table by listing the scores for each animal. Then rate them from first place to sixth place.

	Score	Position
Badger		
Elephant		
Giraffe		
Hedgehog		
Lion		
Tortoise		

95 Fishy business 3

Instead of five ponds with four fish in each, there are four ponds with five fish. Work out the answer to each problem, then choose the odd one out from each pond that needs to be moved into the empty pond.

Tricky

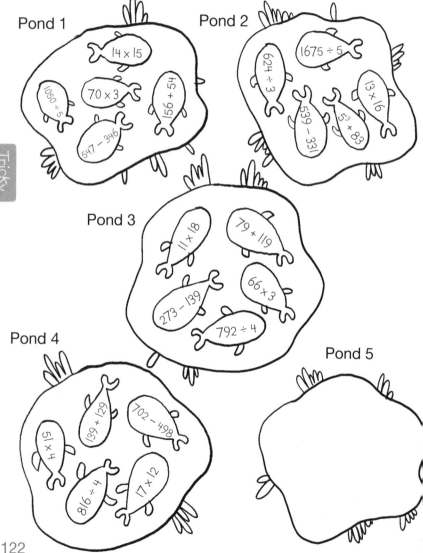

Pond 1

14 × 15
70 × 3
1050 ÷ 5
156 + 54
547 − 346

Pond 2

1675 ÷ 5
624 ÷ 3
539 − 331
5³ + 83
13 × 16

Pond 3

11 × 18
79 + 119
273 − 139
66 × 3
792 ÷ 4

Pond 4

139 + 129
702 − 498
51 × 4
816 ÷ 4
17 × 12

Pond 5

96 Maths sandwiches 3

The café is selling four new maths sandwiches. To make a sandwich there is a number on the top, a number in the filling, in the salad and on the bottom. Each new number is found by following the recipe above each sandwich.

Divide by 17 each time.

Sandwich 1

83521

Add 427 each time.

Sandwich 2

−1125

Subtract 20% each time.

Sandwich 3

1000

Multiply by 1.5 each time.

Sandwich 4

100

Tricky

123

Look at the grid below. Each symbol represents the number 1, 2, 3, 4 or 5. The total for each row is given at the beginning of the row in the grey box. The total for each column is given at the top of the column in the grey box.

Which number does each symbol represent?

	14	13	19	12	16
15	△	⊘	♡	◇	▱
11	⊘	♡	◇	◇	♡
17	▱	⊘	△	▱	♡
13	⊘	▱	△	◇	⊘
18	♡	▱	▱	◇	△

△ ⊘ ♡ ◇ ▱

☐ ☐ ☐ ☐ ☐

Puzzle Pointer

Look for a row or column with a lot of one shape to give you a starting point.

Tricky

124

The grid is locked until the correct numbers are added to the right places. Put the following numbers into the grid so that each number statement is correct.

- The number statements must be correct both vertically and horizontally.

- Each number can only be used once.

16   23   39   39   55   92

	+		=	147
−	■	−	■	−
	+		=	
=	■	=	■	=
	+	69	=	108

Tricky

125

(99) Spinning tops 3

The number in the centre must be reached by
adding all the numbers that are around the outside
of the spinning top. Fill in the missing numbers.

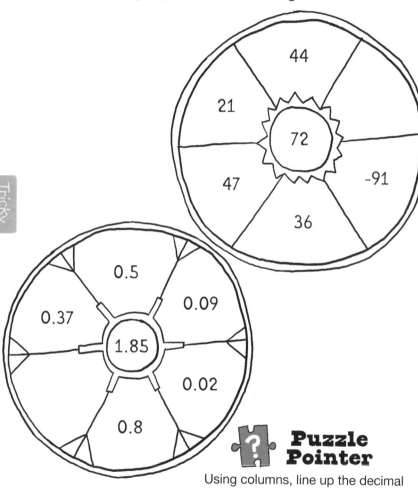

44

21

72

47

-91

36

0.5

0.09

0.37

1.85

0.02

0.8

Puzzle Pointer

Using columns, line up the decimal
points of the numbers you're
adding. Add the numbers in the
same way you would add two-,
three- or four-digit numbers.

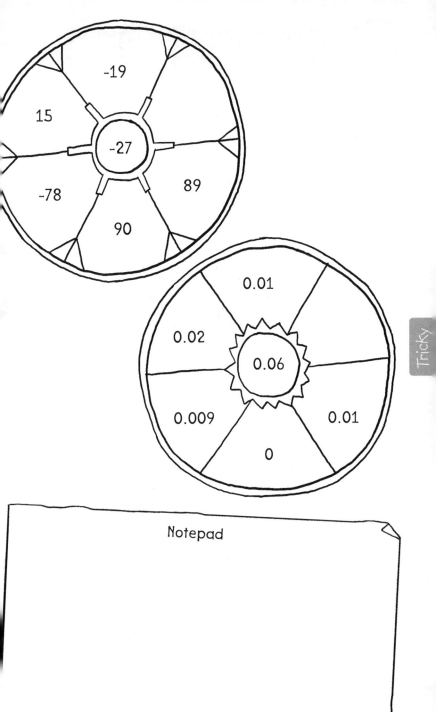

Notepad

(100) Robot pathways 3

Look at the grid map below and then plot the robot as it makes its way around. The first instruction has been done for you.

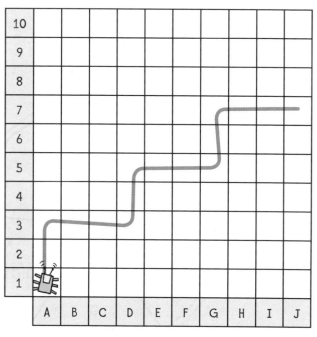

North = N   South = S   East = E   West = W

I begin on A1 and move (N2, E3) three times.

Now I move SW2 three times.

Next, I move (E3, N1) twice.

Then I move (W2, N1, SE2) twice.

After that I move W2.

Finally I move NW6.

Where do I end up?

Tricky

128

101 Number finder 3

Solve the number questions and then find your answers in the number grid. Your answers might be vertical, horizontal or diagonal and should not overlap. The first one has been done for you.

$\frac{1}{2}$ x 4 = _2_

316 + 249 = _____

2431 x 10 = _____

$\frac{3}{4}$ of 32 = _____

562 – 397 = _____

7^2 x 3 = _____

$\frac{2}{3}$ of 360 = _____

815 + 962 = _____

$13^2 + 9^2$ = _____

$\frac{1}{4}$ of 48 = _____

1.2 x 5 = _____

0.5 x 260 = _____

749 – 139 = _____

5^3 x 2^2 = _____

12^2 x 10^2 = _____

Tricky

9	8	1	4	3	1	7	0	0	0	4
6	(2)	1	3	1	0	8	2	4	0	1
5	7	4	2	1	2	7	5	1	0	9
1	6	7	4	6	3	7	5	4	6	2
3	5	2	3	5	0	0	6	4	1	8
2	1	0	1	6	5	3	5	0	0	3
4	8	1	0	5	2	5	0	0	1	7
1	7	7	7	4	1	2	4	3	1	0
5	9	1	9	0	6	7	3	4	2	4

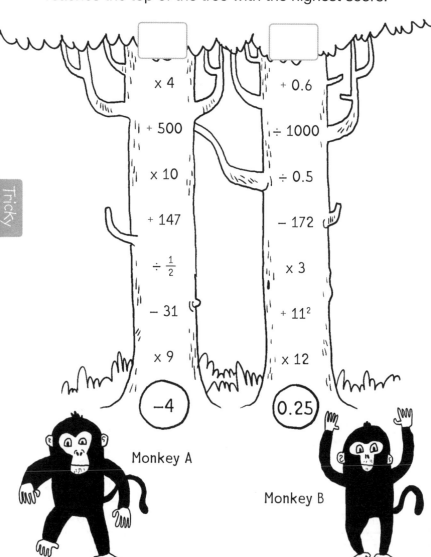

102 Climb the trees 2

Two monkeys are climbing the trees. Follow the maths instructions to find out which monkey reaches the top of the tree with the highest score.

Tricky

Monkey A

× 4

+ 500

× 10

+ 147

÷ $\frac{1}{2}$

− 31

× 9

-4

Monkey B

+ 0.6

÷ 1000

÷ 0.5

− 172

× 3

+ 11^2

× 12

0.25

130

103 Ticking timer

Add three different single-digit numbers together to make a total of 12.

How many ways can you do this?

Here is my ticking timer puzzle. Can you work out the time on my watch using these clues?

- It is an analogue watch (it has two hands and the display is not digital).

- It is in the afternoon.

- The two hands form an almost straight line.

- If I write the time down in number form, the first three numbers are all different, are in size order and form a sequence with the same gap between the digits.

What time is it?

Puzzle Pointer

For the second puzzle, write your answer in 24-hour time.

Notepad

Tricky

131

In the factory there are three rooms. In each room there are a different number of people but they are all doing the same job, making 5000 building blocks. In Rooms 1 and 2, the people are working at the same speed.

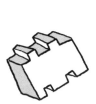
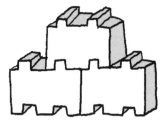

Room 1

Six people take eight hours to make 5000 red building blocks.

Notepad

Tricky

Room 2

Four people are making white building blocks.

How long does it take them to make 5000?

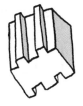

Room 3

Twelve people are making yellow building blocks, but they are using an advanced machine which runs 30% faster.

How long does it take them to make 5000?

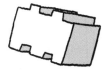

Grace works at a department store where she wraps gifts. Decorate the boxes for her so that:

- 25% have horizontal stripes

- there are half the number of vertical stripes as there are horizontal stripes

- $\frac{3}{8}$ have a check pattern

- the rest of the gift boxes are decorated with a dotted pattern or with a flowery pattern in a 2:3 ratio.

Tricky

Blocks 2

George and Connor have played the blocks game on their computers and the final scores have been revealed. Work out who has won the game using the scoring system below:

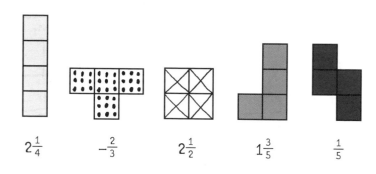

$2\frac{1}{4}$ $-\frac{2}{3}$ $2\frac{1}{2}$ $1\frac{3}{5}$ $\frac{1}{5}$

Tricky

George's Screen   Connor's Screen

 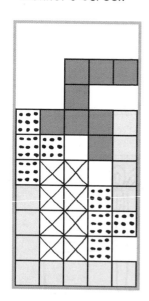

107 Eight point break

All of the balls have a number on them. Draw a line to join any two balls that can be divided to give a score of eight. One has been done for you.

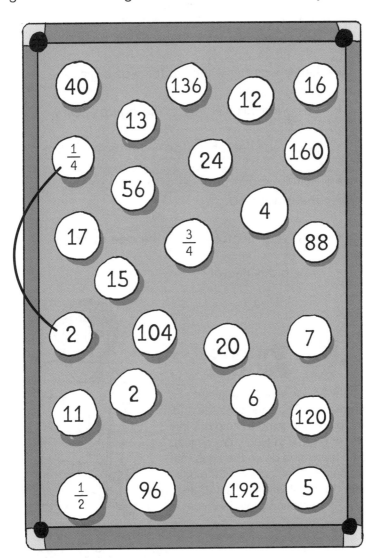

Tricky

137

(108) How old is Hector?

Using this list of facts, work out how old Hector is.

- Lottie was four when Hector was born.

- Archie was six when Hector was born.

- Henry was ten when Hector was born.

- Last year Archie was $\frac{4}{5}$ the age of Henry.

- Next year Hector will be $\frac{1}{4}$ the age of Mum.

- Mum is above the age of 38 and below the age of 60.

- Last year Hector was $\frac{1}{2}$ the age of Henry.

- How old is Hector?

 **Puzzle Pointer**

Always look for the relevant information. The ages of Lottie and Archie are not going to help but the ages of Mum and Henry are critical. Begin by writing down the ages that are possible then cross out the ages that do not fit with the rest of the information provided.

Tricky

Take away one stick to make the equation below correct.

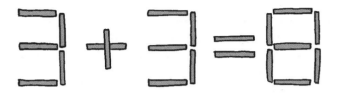

This time take away two sticks to make another correct equation.

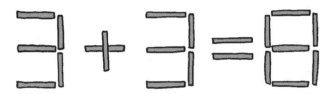

Tricky

Finally, move one stick to a different place to make another correct equation.

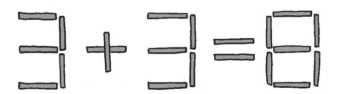

Puzzle Pointer

In each example, no more than one stick should be taken away from one symbol or number.

110 Spider's web

Using a ruler and a pencil, you can make beautiful designs. Pair up the dots that add up to 13 by drawing a straight line. The first one is done for you.

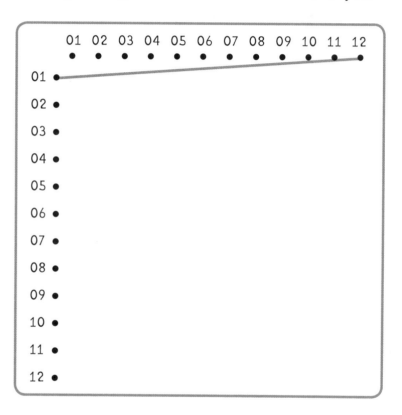

This technique is never ending. You could put numbers and dots all around the square, you could change the square for another shape. You could use sticky tape and thread or pierce holes in black card and use a needle and metallic thread to make beautiful art. Always check with an adult before using a needle.

111 Shut the box

All of the boxes below have a number on the inside lid and each box has a partner box. You can only close a pair of boxes by using a key. The key is the one number that every pair of boxes must add up to.

Find the matching pairs to solve the key and close the boxes. Good luck!

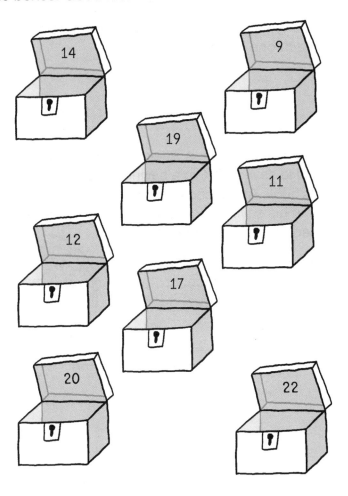

2 is such a small number, but I bet that if I multiply 2 by 2 and keep multiplying the answer by 2, I can get to a million really quickly.

How many times does Meera have to multiply by 2 to reach one million?

Tricky

At the beginning of each week Max gets £2 pocket money. He saves 50% in a savings account and spends 50%. At the end of each week, the money he has in his savings account earns 10% interest (rounded to the nearest penny).

How much money does Max have in his savings account after eight weeks?

Notepad

142

Puzzle power!

Your puzzle power must be nearly at boiling point by now. Check the answers at the end of the book and add up how many tricky puzzles you got right. Score 2 for each fully correct puzzle, and 1 if you got some of the puzzle right. Then write down your total and read on to discover your puzzle power...

My puzzle power score is _____ .

Puzzle power score 1–25

Not bad! Now why not grab a pencil and paper and go over some of the tricky puzzles you found most challenging.

Puzzle power score 26–49

Well done! You have tackled some of the trickiest puzzles in this book. Pop back and see if you can work through some of the puzzles you found difficult.

Puzzle power score 50+

You are a puzzle superstar and there are no limits to your puzzle power! Next stop, see if you can tackle *Bond Brain Training For Kids: Word Puzzles* and *Bond Brain Training For Kids: Logic Puzzles.*

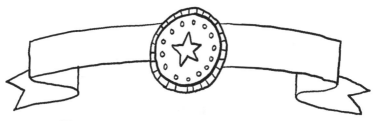

Answers

Warm-up puzzles

PAGE 10

1 Sandcastles 1

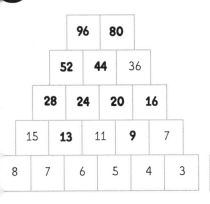

96	80

52	44	36

28	24	20	16

15	13	11	9	7

8	7	6	5	4	3

1	1

4	3	2

12	8	5	3

36	24	16	11	8

98	62	38	22	11	3

PAGE 11

2 Monster maths 1

 = 4   = 3   = 2

 + + = 7

 + + = 8

③ Open the box 1

1. **30**, **35** (This sequence follows the 5 times table.)
2. **57**, **52** (Take away the following to get the next number in the sequence: − 10, − 9, − 8, − 7, − 6, − 5.)
3. **45**, **30** (Take away 15 to get the next number in the sequence.)
4. **64**, **128** (Multiply each number by 2 to get the next number in the sequence.)
5. **49**, **36** (The sequence is square numbers in decreasing order.)
6. **526** then add together the 3 digits (5 + 2 + 6 = 13) leaves us with a prime number. A prime number can only be divided by itself and 1. You should have chosen **Key A**.

④ Zoo numbers

elephant + giraffe (8 + 7) = **15**

spider + snake (6 + 5) = **11**

lion x elephant (4 x 8) = **32**

snake - lion (5 - 4) = **1**

giraffe x spider (7 x 6) = **42**

5 Perfect tens

There are several solutions to this puzzle.
Here is one:

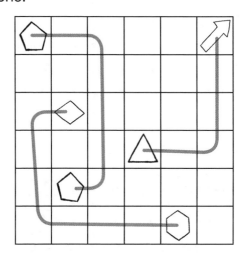

6 Secret codes

The code spells out this joke:

How does a lion greet other animals?

Pleased to eat you!

7 Number ladders 1

1. **50** (412 ÷ 2 = 206 + 44 = 250 ÷ 10 = 25 x 2 = 50)
2. **100** (3 x 100 = 300 + 150 = 450 ÷ 9 = 50 x 2 = 100)
3. **24** (56 ÷ 7 = 8 x 12 = 96 + 48 = 144 ÷ 6 = 24)

8 Hidden numbers 1

1. Go outside i**f our** fire alarm rings.
2. I arrived too so**on e**very morning.
3. We wound the thread on bo**th ree**ls.
4. I don't eat kul**fi ve**ry often but I love the taste of it.
5. What is the w**eight** of these parcels?
6. Check your answer**s even** if you are sure.

9 Shade art 1

2	9	8	28	7	11
39	22	24	36	35	5
3	33	21	30	4	12
5	18	38	80	36	24
24	7	16	18	6	3
17	13	12	24	21	27
9	19	10	15	33	6

10 Mirror mayhem 1

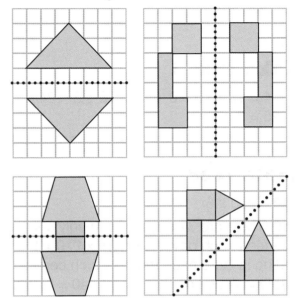

11 Magic square

There is more than one answer to this question.
In every answer, 5 will be the number in the middle.
Here is one solution:

4	9	2
3	5	7
8	1	6

Number riddles 1

PAGE 21

I am **64**; I am **135**.

PAGE 22

Snake sum 1

31 (12 + 4 = 16 − 16 = 0 + 72 = 72 ÷ 3 = 24 + 30 = 54 ÷ 9 = 6 + 25 = 31)

PAGE 23

Stable fees

1. **£1320** (£220 x 6)

2. **£1060** (There are 31 days in both July and August so the feed each day is 62 days x £10 = £620. The boarding is £220 each month which comes to £440. The total calculation is £620 + £440 = £1060.)

3. **£1410** (Begin by working out how much it is for one horse. There are 31 days in December so feed is £10 x 31 = £310 and mucking out is £5 x 31 = £155. Grooming is £20 and boarding is £220. The total calculation is £220 + £310 + £155 + £20 = £705 for each horse. Multiply by 2 = £1410.)

PAGE 24

Futoshiki fun 1

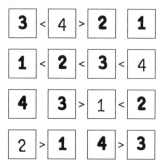

6) Cell crunching 1

	23	7	21
14	9	1	4
17	6	2	9
20	8	4	8

7) Bull's eye 1

20 (12 + 13) – (3 + 2); **3** (11 – 10) + (7 – 5)

8) Cats on hats 1

90 (15 x 6); **52** (13 x 4)

9) Silly sevens

Rose will write down **20** sevens: 7, 17, 27, 37, 47, 57, 67, 70, 71, 72, 73, 74, 75, 76, 77, 78, 79, 87, 97

Byron will need to take **£256** with him. Starting with the £2 he has, we can multiply by 2 to work out how much he had when he went through each tunnel.

Tunnel 7: £2 x 2 = £4, Tunnel 6: £4 x 2 = £8, Tunnel 5: £8 x 2 = £16, Tunnel 4: £16 x 2 = £32, Tunnel 3: £32 x 2 = £64, Tunnel 2: £64 x 2 = £128, Tunnel 1: £128 x 2 = £256

Sudoku fun 1

3	9	1	7	5	4	2	8	6
2	8	7	3	6	1	4	5	9
6	5	4	2	9	8	7	3	1
5	4	8	6	2	3	1	9	7
7	2	9	1	8	5	6	4	3
1	6	3	9	4	7	8	2	5
4	3	6	5	1	2	9	7	8
8	1	5	4	7	9	3	6	2
9	7	2	8	3	6	5	1	4

Nine times table

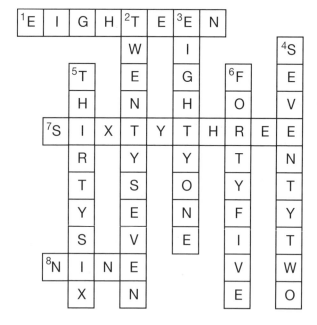

32 Fill the grid 1

	3	5	7	9	5	1	2	
	6					2		
		9	7	6	4	3	1	2
3	6	9			4			5
6			1	8	5	6	2	8
5	1	2	9				3	5
			6		4		4	2
			1	4	7	8	5	2	0

33 Keys and doors 1

48 is $\frac{3}{4}$ of 64   90 is $\frac{3}{4}$ of 120

39 is $\frac{3}{4}$ of 52   84 is $\frac{3}{4}$ of 112

54 is $\frac{3}{4}$ of 72

34 Number train 1

269 people are on the train.

$37 - 29 + 112 - 53 + 96 - 47 + 153 = 269$

157 people are on the train.

$182 - 18 + 72 - 105 + 81 - 96 + 41 = 157$

35 Break the safe

The code is **WELL DONE**.

The answer to Mia's puzzle is the numbers 1, 2 and 3. $(1 \times 2 \times 3 = 6)$ $(1 + 2 + 3 = 6)$

153

Fishy business 1

Pond 1: Each calculation has a total of **42** so **92 + 8** is the odd fish out.

Pond 2: Each calculation has a total of **144** so **25 x 4** is the odd fish out.

Pond 3: Each calculation has a total of **27** so **1000 ÷ 10** is the odd fish out.

Pond 4: Each calculation has a total of **64** so **10²** is the odd fish out.

Pond 5: Each calculation has a total of **100**.

Maths sandwiches 1

Sandwich 1: **96, 48, 24, 12**
(96 ÷ 2 = 48 ÷ 2 = 24 ÷ 2 = 12)
Sandwich 2: **216, 72, 24, 8**
(216 ÷ 3 = 72 ÷ 3 = 24 ÷ 3 = 8)
Sandwich 3: **49, 66, 83, 100**
(49 + 17 = 66 + 17 = 83 + 17 = 100)
Sandwich 4: **5, 25, 125, 625**
(5 x 5 = 25 x 5 = 125 x 5 = 625)

Symbolic sums 1

 = 3   = 2   = 1

39 **Number pyramids 1**

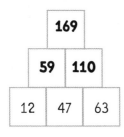

Marion 1: The bottom two numbers are added together to make the number above them.

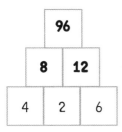

Marion 2: The bottom two numbers are multiplied together to make the number above them.

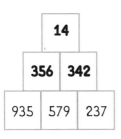

Marion 3: The bottom two numbers are subtracted to make the number above them.

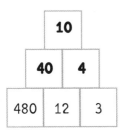

Marion 4: The bottom two numbers are divided to make the number above them. The larger number of the pair is divided by the smaller.

Spinning tops 1

Top with 273 in the centre: the missing number is **93**.

Top with 659 in the centre: the missing number is **217**.

Top with 597 in the centre: the missing number is **82**.

Top with 456 in the centre: the missing number is **39**.

 Birthday bears

1. **Fred Bear** is the oldest.
2. **Daisy Bear** is the youngest.
3. **Brown Bear** is a summer-born bear.
4. **Daisy Bear** was born on 29 February – a leap year day.
5. **Fred Bear and Snowy Bear**'s ages are six months apart.

Robot pathways 1

I end up at **I9**.

33 Number finder 1

$100 \times 10 = \textbf{1000}$ $57 \times 10 = \textbf{570}$ $19 \times 3 = \textbf{57}$

$512 \div 8 = \textbf{64}$ $144 \div 12 = \textbf{12}$ $450 \div 5 = \textbf{90}$

$712 + 509 = \textbf{1221}$ $31 + 287 = \textbf{318}$ $432 + 59 = \textbf{491}$

$876 - 543 = \textbf{333}$ $753 - 246 = \textbf{507}$ $139 - 86 = \textbf{53}$

3	4	5	7	0	3	0	2
2	1	8	6	4	1	3	4
1	5	0	5	9	8	3	7
2	0	8	0	7	0	3	6
4	7	5	3	0	4	9	1
7	1	2	2	1	2	3	9

34 Bunny hop race

Honey Bunny: (+ 5, − 2) 0, 5, 3, **8, 6, 11, 9, 14, 12, 17, 15, 20, 18, 23, 21, 26**

Sunny Bunny: (+ 7, − 5) 0, 7, 2, **9, 4, 11, 6, 13, 8, 15, 10, 17, 12, 19, 14, 21**

Funny Bunny: (+ 8, − 4) 0, 8, 4, **12, 8, 16, 12, 20, 16, 24, 20, 28, 24, 32, 28, 36**

Funny Bunny wins the race.

How many?

Alex can make 20 complete pencil cases.

He has 12 metres (m) of green fabric and he needs 50 centimetres (cm) for each case so 1200 cm ÷ 50 cm = 24 pencil cases.

He has 5 m of white fabric and he needs 20 cm for each case so 500 cm ÷ 20 cm = 25 pencil cases.

He has 3 m of brown fabric and he needs 15 cm for each case so 300 cm ÷ 15 cm = 20 pencil cases.

He has enough zips for 40 pencil cases.

 # Funny fours

Card 1: **A = 17** (B = 16); Card 2: **B = 16** (A = 15);
Card 3: **B = 20** (A = 18)

 # Hot-air balloons

3 ($\frac{1}{12}$ of 36) balloons have vertical stripes.

9 (36 ÷ 4) balloons have wavy lines.

6 ($\frac{1}{6}$ of 36) balloons have a dotted pattern.

12 (36 ÷ 3) balloons are plain white.

6 (36 – 3 – 9 – 6 – 12) balloons have horizontal stripes.

PAGES 54–5

58 **Monkey maze**

Monkey D is the winner.

12	**3**	13	15	56	55	60	45	**5**	9
33	9	18	80	65	40	29	38	15	19
15	24	27	6	30	79	80	46	35	29
2	87	40	34	31	51	62	72	20	75
16	28	31	26	29	37	52	62	47	95
34	19	20					12	52	80
10	14	35					29	36	61
52	70	13					14	31	92
69	56	51	68	57	46	26	19	71	86
9	35	84	77	49	14	17	23	31	24
12	21	11	81	30	42	35	67	19	13
36	26	39	46	12	43	21	31	46	4
18	**6**	24	60	72	29	63	28	**7**	15

Monster maths 2

 = 13   = 7   = 17

 + + (monster) = 37

(monster) + (monster) + (monster) = 43

Fifty point break

38 is the ball that does not have a pair.

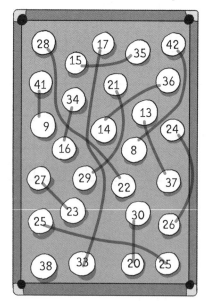

41 Zoo link words

```
                              T  O  A  D
         K  A  N  G  A  R  O  O
            P                 R        Z
      C  H  E  E  T  A  H     T        E
      A                       O        B
      M  O  N  K  E  Y        I        R
      E                       S  E  A  L
   E  L  E  P  H  A  N  T      E        I
                     I                  Z
         L           G                  A
      G  I  R  A  F  F  E     B  E  A  R
         O           R                  D
   P  E  N  G  U  I  N
```

1	2	3	5	6	8	9	10	11	12	16
E	O	N	M	K	L	H	S	Y	F	R

17	18	19	20	21	22	23	24	25	26
G	I	T	B	C	Z	D	U	A	P

PAGE 59

42 Perfect 14s

Here is one possible solution to the puzzle.

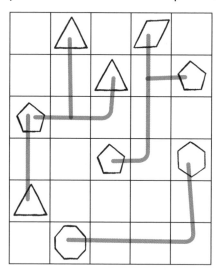

PAGE 60

43 Number ladders 2

1. **1250** (1000 ÷ 10 = 100 + 25 = 125 x 5 = 625 x 2 = 1250)
2. **240** (32 x 4 = 128 + 52 = 180 ÷ 3 = 60 x 4 = 240)
3. **24** (40 – 8 = 32 x 3 = 96 + 48 = 144 ÷ 6 = 24)

PAGE 61

44 Hidden numbers 2

1. Who would no**t wo**nder why it was snowing in summer?
2. That chair has the com**fort y**ou need.
3. The little mouse a**te n**ervously, always watchful.

4. I left the paper in the loft and i**t went y**ellow.

5. I reached the hot**el even**tually, tired and hungry.

6. The secretarie**s even ty**ped the letter for me. (**seven** or **seventy** are both correct)

The answer to the extra puzzle is: **Leo**.

PAGE 62

 ## Cross out

There is more than one answer to these questions. Here are some examples:

A pair that add up to a square number = **31 + 18** (49)

A pair that add up to a prime number = **37 + 4** (41)

A pair that add up to the product of 3 and 5 = **3 + 12** (15)

A pair that add up to 100 = **42 + 58**

PAGE 63

 ## Shade art 2

2	48	12	44	14	40	8	32	53	42
46	30	34	20	26	24	38	51	22	50
38	31	10	25	16	4	48	15	46	2
12	1	26	18	81	29	22	16	26	51
44	24	14	28	6	8	50	3	54	30
34	8	36	45	2	44	14	25	12	34
22	29	21	32	40	20	38	4	50	22
30	4	41	29	10	36	32	31	2	48
48	12	42	26	44	50	18	42	52	24
14	38	20	34	8	46	24	40	30	18

PAGE 64

Mirror mayhem 2

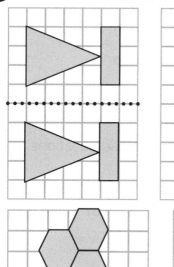

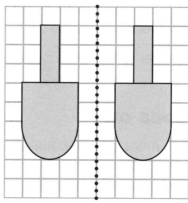

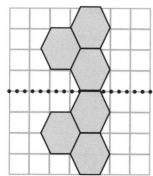

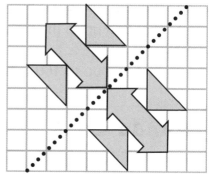

PAGE 65

Number riddles 2

I am **169**; I am **248**.

PAGE 66

Snake sum 2

155 (56 + 4 = 60 − 25 = 35 + 121 = 156 ÷ 3 = 52 + 47 = 99 ÷ 9 = 11 + 144 = 155)

50 Sandcastles 2

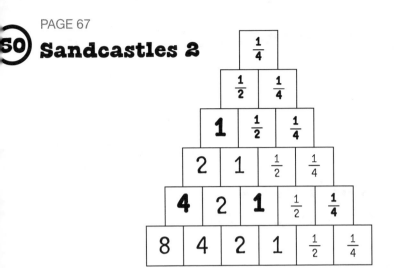

51 Grabber machine

Zara has the most valuable collection of teddy bears.
(Zara has 2 x £3, 2 x £2, 2 x £1.50 and 3 x £1 = £16.
Charlie has 2 x £3, 1 x £2, 2 x £1.50 and 4 x £1 = £15)

52 Futoshiki fun 2

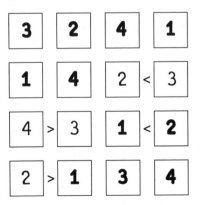

PAGE 71

53 Cell crunching 2

	6	16	20
20	3	**8**	**9**
15	**2**	**6**	**7**
7	**1**	**2**	**4**

PAGE 72

54 Bull's eye 2

450 (15 x 3) x (12 − 2); **60** (12 ÷ 4) x (9 + 11)

PAGE 73

55 Cats on hats 2

Divide the number to the left of the hat by the number to the right of the hat and add the number below the hat.

13 (121 ÷ 11) + 2

PAGE 74

56 Sudoku fun 2

6	1	**9**	**7**	4	**2**	8	**3**	5
7	5	**8**	3	9	**1**	2	6	**4**
4	3	2	8	**5**	6	7	9	**1**
5	2	6	9	**1**	3	4	**8**	7
8	9	4	**5**	2	**7**	3	1	6
1	7	**3**	6	8	**4**	**5**	**2**	**9**
2	**8**	1	4	6	5	**9**	7	3
9	4	7	1	3	**8**	**6**	**5**	2
3	**6**	5	**2**	7	9	1	4	8

Fill the grid 2

	9	7	5	3	2	4	6		
	1					0			
		5	7	9	3	1	0		7
6	7	9				6			4
7				1	5	8	9	1	6
3	2	5		3				9	5
				5		4		2	5
				7	9	2	6	8	3	1

 Groups of 25

9	7	8	7	5	5	1	2	2	4
9	4	5	5	3	5	1	5	3	4
1	3	3	3	4	5	9	8	6	3
2	4	2	6	5	5	5	7	6	6
4	5	1	2	1	6	7	1	1	6
6	8	1	2	1	2	1	9	3	1
4	3	3	5	1	5	6	5	6	2
4	5	4	4	4	4	4	4	1	6
5	7	6	6	1	4	3	4	1	5
9	5	5	2	7	6	5	2	3	4

PAGE 77

(59) Keys and doors 2

$\frac{12}{20} = 0.6$ $\frac{6}{8} = 0.75$ $\frac{6}{24} = 0.25$ $\frac{24}{30} = 0.8$ $\frac{9}{20} = 0.45$

PAGE 78

(60) Number train 2

683 people are on the train.

$149 - 71 + 162 - 53 + 239 - 57 + 314 = 683$

214 people are on the train.

$437 - 218 + 112 - 196 + 68 - 85 + 96 = 214$

PAGE 79

(61) Fishy business 2

Pond 1: Each calculation has a total of 49 so **4 x 12 = 48** is the odd fish out.

Pond 2: Each calculation has a total of 35 so **72 ÷ 2 = 36** is the odd fish out.

Pond 3: Each calculation has a total of 25 so **3 x 8 = 24** is the odd fish out.

Pond 4: Each calculation has a total of 66 so **6^2 ÷ 3 = 12** is the odd fish out.

Pond 5: The answer to each calculation is in the **12 times table** (12, 24, 36, 48)

All of the fish in pond 5 are in the 12 times table.

PAGES 80–1

62 Who ate the fish?

The codes say:

**Is it Hungry Horace? Is it Famished Fluffy?
Is it Starving Sooty? Is it Greedy Gigi?
Is it Ravenous Ragtail?**

The guilty cat is Famished Fluffy.

PAGE 82

63 Maths sandwiches 2

Sandwich 1: **320, 80, 20, 5**

$(320 ÷ 4 = 80 ÷ 4 = 20 ÷ 4 = 5)$

Sandwich 2: **597, 480, 363, 246**

$(597 - 117 = 480 – 117 = 363 – 117 = 246)$

Sandwich 3: **543, 1086, 2172, 4344**

$(543 × 2 = 1086 × 2 = 2172 × 2 = 4344)$

Sandwich 4: **800, 1200, 1800, 2700**

$(800 + 400 = 1200 + 600 = 1800 + 900 = 2700)$

PAGE 83

64 Symbolic sums 2

 = 4   ▮ = 2   = 1   ♡ = 3

In the third column we have 3 crosses and 1 trapezium to make 5. So we have 1 + 1 + 1 + 2. If we then look at the bottom row, we have 3 trapeziums and 1 circle to make 10, so if a trapezium is worth 2 then a circle is worth 4. If we now look at the first column, we know that a trapezium is worth 2, so heart is worth 3.

Number pyramids 2

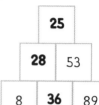

Harry 1: The bottom two numbers are subtracted to find the number above.

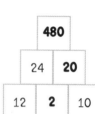

Harry 2: The bottom two numbers are multiplied to find the number above.

66 Number finder 2

$47 \times 3 = \mathbf{141}$	$27 \times 4 = \mathbf{108}$	$560 \div 8 = \mathbf{70}$
$169 \div 13 = \mathbf{13}$	$5^3 = \mathbf{125}$	$15 \times 5 = \mathbf{75}$
$136 + 249 = \mathbf{385}$	$987 + 132 = \mathbf{1119}$	$23 \times 6 = \mathbf{138}$
$963 - 246 = \mathbf{717}$	$29 \times 10 = \mathbf{290}$	$846 \div 3 = \mathbf{282}$

7	1	7	7	1	2	9	3
1	3	6	5	3	9	1	8
9	8	1	4	1	0	0	5
1	1	1	9	5	1	8	6
3	7	2	8	2	2	9	4
2	0	1	3	8	5	0	5

Spinning tops 2

Top with 811 in the centre: the missing number is **217**.

Top with 321 in the centre: the missing number is **11**.

Top with 5 in the centre: the missing number is **–7**.

Top with 2 in the centre: the missing number is **0.93**.

68 Gridlock 1

6	+	4	=	10
+		–		÷
2	×	1	=	2
=		=		=
8	–	3	=	5

The answer to the boy's puzzle is **336** legs altogether.

Robot pathways 2

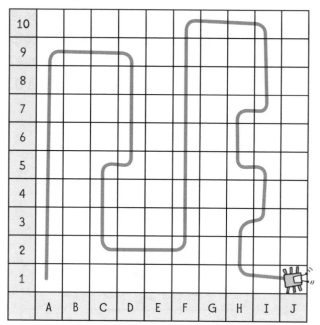

The robot ends up at **J1**.

 Climb the trees 1

Monkey A: 12 x 7 = 84 + 29 = 113 x 2 = 226 + 23 = 249 ÷ 3 = 83 – 25 = 58 x 4 = **232**

Monkey B: 12 ÷ 4 = 3 + 25 = 28 x 2 = 56 + 47 = 103 – 4 = 99 x 10 = 990 ÷ 3 = **330**

Monkey B has the higher score.

172

 **Blocks 1**

Pavith has won. (Pavith has 2 x 10 = 20;
2 x 15 = 30; 2 x 12 = 24; 1 x 20 = 20; 1 x 25 = 25.
Total = 119 points)

(Kareen has 1 x 10 = 10; 1 x 15 = 15; 2 x 12 = 24;
2 x 20 = 40; 1 x 25 = 25. Total = 114 points)

 Sew confused

They all work for 7 hours – 1 hour for lunch = 6 hours.

Lizzy makes 2 covers an hour: every o'clock and
every half past the hour (6 x 2 = 12 covers).

Ashley makes 3 covers an hour: every 20 and 40
minutes past and o'clock (6 x 3 = 18 covers).

Madison makes 4 covers an hour: every 15, 30, 45
minutes past and o'clock, (6 x 4 = 24 covers).

1. In 6 hours they make a total of **54 covers**.

2. Every o'clock they complete a cover at the same
   time = **6 times**.

3. Lizzy and Ashley finish a cover every o'clock at the
   same time = **6 times**.

4. Lizzy and Madison finish a cover every o'clock and
   half past = **12 times**.

73 ## Jazzy reindeer

10 reindeer antler covers have horizontal stripes.

3 reindeer antler covers have vertical stripes.

5 reindeer antler covers have a dotted pattern.

6 reindeer antler covers have a criss-crossed pattern.

6 reindeer antler covers are plain white.

Tricky puzzles

74 ## Monster maths 3

 = 8   = 6   = 7

 + + = 21

 × × = 336

75) Swinging on a star

Four times table.

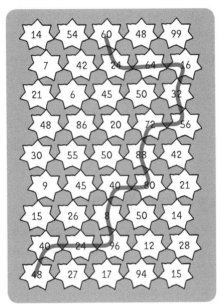

76) Number ladders 3

1. **1.2** ($512 \div 64 = 8 \times 0.5 = 4 \div 10 = 0.4 \times 3 = 1.2$)
2. **–6** ($63 - 100 = -37 \times 2 = -74 + 50 = -24 \times 0.25 = -6$)
3. **0** ($0 + 0.75 = 0.75 \times 5 = 3.75 \div 3 = 1.25 - 1.25 = 0$)

77) Open the box 2

1. **41, 12** (– 29 to get to the next number in the sequence.)
2. **38, 11** (– 27 to get to the next number in the sequence.)

3. **34, 55** (The pattern is a Fibonacci sequence: the first number + the second number = the third number.)

4. **75, 76** (– 10 to get to the next number, then + 1 to get to the next number. Alternate this pattern.)

5. **27, 8** (The sequence is cubed numbers.)

6. If you add up the answers, the three-digit number you will make is: **377**.

7. If you add up the three digits you get 17. This is not a triangular number, so you need to circle **Key B**.

PAGES 102–3

 Funny numbers

Nish adds a decimal point to make 4.6.

Yes, every party bag Jasmine is making can be different.

(3 x 4 x 5 = 60 and Jasmine needs 45 bags.)

The tortoise is 94.

(The tortoise's 25th birthday was egg laying year 1 + 13 other times she laid eggs. 25 years old + (13 x 5) = 90. The next time she will lay eggs will be next year so it is 4 years since the last time she laid eggs. The tortoise is 94 years old.)

Zara thought of the number 49.

To solve this write down all of the possible answers that are 2 away (39, 43, 45, 49, 51, 55, 59, 63, 66, 70). Then cross out the answers that are NOT also 4 away (leaving: 43, 45, 49, 51). Then those that are NOT also 8 away (leaving: 45, 49), or 12 away (leaving only 49). Now we know that Zara's number is 49.

79 Shade art 3

1	4	29	9	64	16	23	8
49	10	25	15	52	86	20	64
64	15	31	48	100	27	60	19
27	6	81	14	4	8	42	11
81	24	9	26	54	68	56	23
3	20	2	49	125	16	28	17
8	52	25	16	19	7	14	81
36	38	8	5	1	49	40	8
7	30	27	7	3	25	6	29
64	5	25	8	2	11	37	13

30 Mirror butterfly

Riddle: The number is 7 (S) E V E N!

PAGE 106

(81) Number riddles 3

I am **864**; I am **23532**.

PAGE 107

(82) Snake sum 3

−3 (60 + 196 = 256 ÷ 8 = 32 − 45 = −13 x 10 = −130 + 64 = −66 x 0.5 = −33 ÷ 11 = −3)

PAGE 108

(83) Shape-shifter

 = 5   = 10

Use algebra to solve this puzzle so that square = S and hexagon = H like this:

$3S + H = 25$ $3H + S = 35$

One statement has 3S. The other has 3H. If we multiply either of these statements by 3, we can then subtract the expressions that are the same, like this:

$3S + H = 25$ (x 3) = $9S + 3H = 75$

$S + 3H = 35$

$8S = 40$ so $S = 5$

Now substitute this in any of the initial expressions to find H: $3H + 5 = 35$ (now − 5)

$3H = 30$ so $H = 10$

These are called simultaneous equations.

84 Sandcastles 3

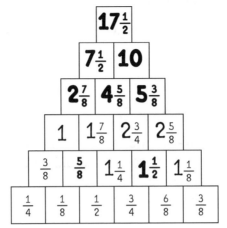

$17\frac{1}{2}$

$7\frac{1}{2}$ | 10

$2\frac{7}{8}$ | $4\frac{5}{8}$ | $5\frac{3}{8}$

1 | $1\frac{7}{8}$ | $2\frac{3}{4}$ | $2\frac{5}{8}$

$\frac{3}{8}$ | $\frac{5}{8}$ | $1\frac{1}{4}$ | $1\frac{1}{2}$ | $1\frac{1}{8}$

$\frac{1}{4}$ | $\frac{1}{8}$ | $\frac{1}{2}$ | $\frac{3}{4}$ | $\frac{6}{8}$ | $\frac{3}{8}$

85 Futoshiki fun 3

4	2 < 3	1
1	4	2	3
3	1	4 > 2
2	3 > 1	4

86 Cell crunching 3

	32	43	57
75	15	29	31
31	9	8	14
26	8	6	12

PAGE 112

87 Bull's eye 3

74 (15 x 5) − (9 − 8) = 74 OR (15 x 5) − 9 + 8 = 74
24 (15 ÷ 15) x (13 + 11) = 24

PAGE 113

88 Cats on hats 3

Divide the number to the left of the hat by the number to the right of the hat. Multiply the answer by the number below the hat.

2.4 (30 ÷ 25) x 2

PAGE 114

89 Sudoku fun 3

7	2	5	3	8	6	9	1	4
8	4	3	1	2	9	7	5	6
9	6	1	5	7	4	3	8	2
4	3	9	2	5	1	8	6	7
1	7	2	4	6	8	5	3	9
6	5	8	7	9	3	2	4	1
5	9	6	8	4	7	1	2	3
3	8	7	6	1	2	4	9	5
2	1	4	9	3	5	6	7	8

90 Mixed times tables

Across: 1. TWENTYEIGHT 3. TWELVE 4. FIVE 7. FOUR 8. THIRTYSIX 9. FIFTEEN 10. SEVENTYTWO

Down: 1. TWENTYFIVE 2. TWENTYSEVEN 5. EIGHTYONE 6. SIXTEEN 7. FORTYFIVE

91 Fill the grid 3

	4	2	6	1	3	6	9	
1		4	2	3	6	0		8
2	3		9	5	1		5	0
9	3	7		7		6	3	7
8	4	8		2		5	4	2
5	4		7	4	1		9	4
6		8	3	6	7	5		1
	2	8	3	8	3	8	2	

Keys and doors 3

$\frac{3}{30} = 0.1 \div 2 = \mathbf{0.05}$ $\frac{48}{40} = 1.2 \div 2 = \mathbf{0.6}$

$\frac{14}{20} = 0.7 \div 2 = \mathbf{0.35}$ $\frac{16}{100} = 0.16 \div 2 = \mathbf{0.08}$

$\frac{8}{5} = 1.6 \div 2 = \mathbf{0.8}$

 Products and sums

Hedgehog	5
Badger	9
Tortoise	3
Giraffe	6
Elephant	4

To solve this question, work out the possible factors like this:

Hedgehog × Badger has a product of 45 so the factors of 45 are: 1 × 45, 3 × 15, 5 × 9.

If you now look at a pair of these factors that also has a sum of 14, then Hedgehog and Badger have the number 5 and the number 9.

Tortoise × Giraffe has a product of 18 so the factors are: 1 × 18, 2 × 9, 3 × 6.

For a sum of 9, Tortoise and Giraffe have the numbers 3 and 6.

Elephant × Hedgehog × Tortoise has a product of 60 but we can include the numbers we already know and we can use the letter E to represent the elephant:

E × 9 × 3 = 60. This must be incorrect as 9 is not a factor of 60.

E × 5 × 6 = 60
   E = 2 (2 + 5 + 6 = 13 so this is incorrect)

E × 9 × 6 = 60. This must be incorrect as 9 is not a factor of 60.

E × 5 × 3 = 60
   E = 4 (4 + 5 + 3 = 12 so this is correct)

You now know that Hedgehog has the 5, Badger has the 9, Tortoise has the 3, Giraffe has the 6 and Elephant has the 4.

You can check this with the last group. T × B × E has a product (3 × 9 × 4) of 108 and the sum (3 + 9 + 4) of 16.

PAGES 120–1

94) Animal of the Year

	Score	Position
Badger	90.7	6th
Elephant	107.2	2nd
Giraffe	90.8	5th
Hedgehog	103.9	3rd
Lion	98.4	4th
Tortoise	108.9	1st

Fishy business 3

Pond 1: Each calculation has a total of 210 so
547 – 346 = 201 is the odd fish out.

Pond 2: Each calculation has a total of 208 so
1675 ÷ 5 = 335 is the odd fish out.

Pond 3: Each calculation has a total of 198 so
273 – 139 = 134 is the odd fish out.

Pond 4: Each calculation has a total of 204 so
139 + 129 = 268 is the odd fish out.

Pond 5: Each calculation in this pond is **a multiple of 67** (134, 201, 268, 335).

 # Maths sandwiches 3

Sandwich 1: **83521, 4913, 289, 17**
(83521 ÷ 17 = 4913 ÷ 17 = 289 ÷ 17 =17)
Sandwich 2: **–1125, –698, –271, 156**
(–1125 + 427 = –698 + 427 = –271 + 427 = 156)
Sandwich 3: **1000, 800, 640, 512**
(1000 – 200 = 800 – 160 = 640 – 128 = 512)
Sandwich 4: **100, 150, 225, 337.5**
(100 x 1.5 = 150 x 1.5 = 225 x 1.5 = 337.5)

 # Symbolic sums 3

 = 5   = 1   = 3   = 2   = 4

PAGE 125

Gridlock 2

55		92		147
–	■	–	■	–
16		23		39
	■		■	
39		69		108

PAGES 126–7

Spinning tops 3

Top with 72 in the centre: the missing number is **15**.

Top with 1.85 in the centre: the missing number is **0.07**.

Top with –27 in the centre: the missing number is **–124**.

Top with 0.06 in the centre: the missing number is **0.011**.

100 Robot pathways 3

I end up at **B7**.

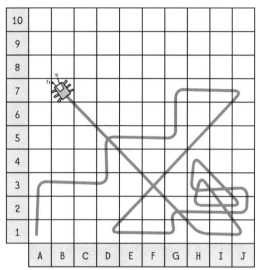

101 Number finder 3

$\frac{1}{2}$ x 4 = **2**   316 + 249 = **565**   2431 x 10 = **24310**

$\frac{3}{4}$ of 32 = **24**   562 – 397 = **165** 7^2 x 3 = **147**

$\frac{2}{3}$ of 360 = **240**   815 + 962 = **1777** $13^2 + 9^2$ = **250**

$\frac{1}{4}$ of 48 = **12**   1.2 x 5 = **6**   0.5 x 260 = **130**

749 – 139 = **610** 5^3 x 2^2 = **500** 12^2 x 10^2 = **14400**

9	8	1	4	3	1	7	0	0	0	4
0	2	1	3	1	0	8	2	4	0	1
5	7	4	2	1	2	7	5	1	0	9
1	6	7	4	0	3	7	5	4	6	2
3	5	2	3	5	0	0	6	4	1	8
0	1	0	1	6	5	3	5	0	0	3
4	8	1	0	5	2	5	0	0	1	7
1	7	7	7	4	1	2	4	3	1	0
5	9	1	9	0	4	7	3	4	0	4

PAGE 130

02 Climb the trees 2

Monkey A: $-4 \times 9 = -36 - 31 = -67 \div \frac{1}{2} = -134 + 147$
$= 13 \times 10 = 130 + 500 = 630 \times 4 = \textbf{2520}$.

Monkey B: $0.25 \times 12 = 3 + 121 = 124 \times 3 = 372 - 172$
$= 200 \div 0.5 = 400 \div 1000 = 0.4 + 0.6 = \textbf{1}$.

Monkey A has the higher score.

PAGE 131

03 Ticking timer

There are **seven** ways to add three different single-digit numbers together to make a total of 12: (1, 2, 9), (1, 3, 8), (1, 4, 7), (1, 5, 6), (2, 3, 7), (2, 4, 6), (3, 4, 5)

The time on the watch is **12.30**. The hour hand of the clock moves gradually so the line is not exactly straight.

Factory fun

Room 1: 8 hours (6 people take 8 hours = it takes a total of 48 hours to make 5000 blocks.)

Room 2: If it takes 48 hours to make 5000 blocks then 48 hours ÷ 4 people = **12 hours**.

Room 3: 12 people would take 4 hours if they worked at the same speed as the other rooms (48 hours ÷ 12 people = 4 hours). This is 240 minutes. 30% of 240 minutes = 72 minutes (10% of 240 = 24 so 30% is 24 x 3 = 72). 240 minutes – 72 minutes = **168 minutes or 2 hours and 48 minutes**.

 Gift boxes

10 boxes have horizontal stripes.

5 boxes have vertical stripes.

15 boxes have a check pattern.

4 boxes have a dotted pattern.

6 boxes have a flowery pattern.

 Blocks 2

Connor has won.

George has $2 \times -\frac{2}{3} = -1\frac{1}{3}$; $3 \times 2\frac{1}{2} = 7\frac{1}{2}$; $2 \times \frac{1}{5} = \frac{2}{5}$; $2 \times 1\frac{3}{5} = 3\frac{1}{5}$. Total = $9\frac{23}{30}$ points.

Connor has $3 \times 2\frac{1}{4} = 6\frac{3}{4}$; $2 \times -\frac{2}{3} = -1\frac{1}{3}$; $2 \times 2\frac{1}{2} = 5$; $2 \times 1\frac{3}{5} = 3\frac{1}{5}$. Total = $13\frac{37}{60}$ points.

07 Eight point break

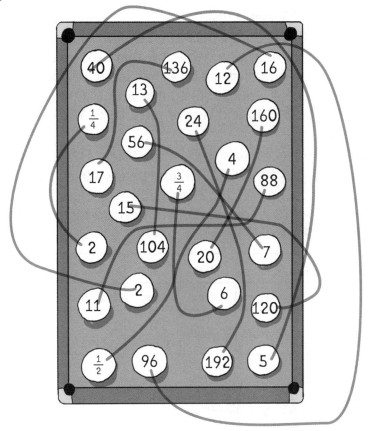

$2 \div \frac{1}{4} = 8$; $96 \div 12 = 8$; $136 \div 17 = 8$; $4 \div \frac{1}{2} = 8$;
$104 \div 13 = 8$; $88 \div 11 = 8$; $6 \div \frac{3}{4} = 8$; $192 \div 24 = 8$;
$16 \div 2 = 8$; $160 \div 20 = 8$; $56 \div 7 = 8$; $120 \div 15 = 8$;
$40 \div 5 = 8$

How old is Hector?

Hector is 11 years old.

To solve this you can start with Hector being $\frac{1}{4}$ the age of Mum **next** year. We know that next year Mum must be an age divisible by 4. Her possible age **next** year is (40, 44, 48, 52, 56) so this year Mum must be 39, 43, 47, 51, 55 and Hector must be 9, 10, 11, 12, 13.

Last year Hector was $\frac{1}{2}$ the age of Henry so Henry must be (16, 18, 20, 22, 24) **last** year so this year Henry must be (17, 19, 21, 23, 25). You know that Henry was 10 when Hector was born so there must be a difference of 10 years.

HECTOR	9	10	**11**	12	13
HENRY	17	19	**21**	23	25
Age difference	8 years	9 years	**10 years**	11 years	12 years

 Moving sticks

$$3 + 3 = 6$$

$$3 - 3 = 0$$

$$5 + 3 = 8$$

10 Spider's web

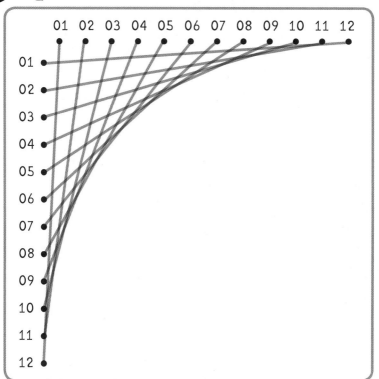

11 Shut the box

Each box should add up to **31**.

(14 + 17), (9 + 22), (20 + 11), (12 + 19)

Mad multiples

If Meera begins with the number 2 and multiplies by 2 each time, she only needs to do this **19 times** before reaching a million!

After eight weeks Max has saved **£12.57** (rounded each time).

Week 1: £1 + 10% = £1.10
Week 2: £1.10 + £1 + 10% = £2.31
Week 3: £2.31 + £1 + 10% = £3.64
Week 4: £3.64 + £1 + 10% = £5.10
Week 5: £5.10 + £1 + 10% = £6.71
Week 6: £6.71 + £1 + 10% = £8.48
Week 7: £8.48 + £1 + 10% = £10.43
Week 8: £10.43 + £1 + 10% = £12.57